DON'T CALL IT ART

10 WAYS TO CREATE LIKE A KID AGAIN

AUSTIN KLEON

WITH DRAWINGS BY OWEN + JULES KLEON

TARCHER
an imprint of Penguin Random House
New York

Tarcher
an imprint of Penguin Random House LLC
1745 Broadway, New York, NY 10019
penguinrandomhouse.com

Book design by Austin Kleon and Shannon Nicole Plunkett

Cover design by Austin Kleon

LIBRARY OF CONGRESS CATALOGING-IN-PUBLICATION DATA

Names: Kleon, Austin author
Title: Don't call it art
Description: New York: Tarcher, [2026]
Identifiers: LCCN 2025051105 (print) | LCCN 2025051106 (ebook) |
ISBN 9798217047888 hardcover | ISBN 9798217047895 ebook
Subjects: LCSH: Creation (Literary, artistic, etc.)
Classification: LCC BH301.C84 K59 2026 (print) |
LCC BH301.C84 (ebook) | DDC 153.3/5—dc23/eng/20260126
LC record available at https://lccn.loc.gov/2025051105
LC ebook record available at https://lccn.loc.gov/2025051106

Printed in Canada
9 8 7 6 5 4 3 2 1

The authorized representative in the EU for product safety and compliance is Penguin Random House Ireland, Morrison Chambers, 32 Nassau Street, Dublin D02 YH68, Ireland, https://eu-contact.penguin.ie.

FOR THE KID IN YOU

CONTENTS

"I LEARNED SO MUCH ABOUT ART FROM WATCHING A KID DRAW... KIDS **DON'T CALL IT ART** WHEN THEY'RE THROWING THINGS AROUND, DRAWING— THEY'RE JUST DOING STUFF."

—JOHN BALDESSARI (1931–2020)

THIS IS A BOOK OF ART LESSONS I LEARNED FROM MY CREATIVE KIDS.

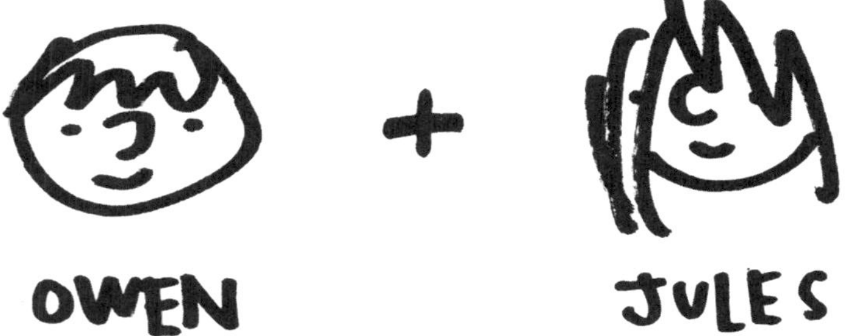

"People do much better when they don't think they're being artists . . . if you don't call it art, you're likely to get a better result."

—BRIAN ENO

I never went to art school, but being around my kids was more inspiring than any art school I can imagine. By the time my boys were toddlers, they drew like two pint-sized Picassos. They worked the way I dreamed of working: without fear or hesitation, just wild energy, raw passion, and a lightness of touch.

They schooled me, all right—you could even say they *unschooled* me. I had assumed, as their dad and the author of *Steal Like an Artist* and other books about creativity that have sold millions of copies around the world, that I would be their teacher and they would be my students. It soon became clear that the opposite was true: I had way more to learn from them than they had to learn from me.

So, I apprenticed myself to beginners. I was the studio assistant now, and things went smoothly as long as I knew my place. My job was to fetch art supplies, fix snacks, and soothe tantrums. Anytime I tried to give them pointers or tell them what to do, it backfired on me. I learned to keep my mouth shut and my eyes open. Occasionally, they let me join the fun, but they certainly didn't need anybody to teach them how to be creative. What they needed was for me to be there when called upon but otherwise stay out of their way.

Whenever I shared the stuff they made online, readers kept asking me when I was going to write a book about creativity for kids.

"Kids don't need a book!" I'd protest. "We need a book so we can be more like them!"

This is that book.

when

the

future comes

all

Experts

become

students

As I was learning to love and care for these little artists in my life, I started wondering why I didn't show myself the same love and care. It was the thought I had when I read parenting books: Why are we doing all this stuff for our kids but not ourselves? Why aren't we *all* taking time to play? Why aren't we *all* letting ourselves get bored? Why aren't we *all* limiting our screen time and going outside?

One day I was listening to an interview with the musician Fiona Apple, and she admitted that she reads a lot of parenting books, not because she plans on having kids but because she wants to learn how to parent *herself*. "So, you're the parent and the child?" the interviewer asked.

"Well, I mean, you always have to be," Apple said. "Everybody has to be for themselves, I think."

In this book, I'm going to help you learn how to treat yourself with the care of a loving parent so that the wild, creative kid who still lives in you can come out and play.

I want to emphasize here that you do not need to have kids or want to have kids or even *like* kids to read this book! But if you do have kids in your life, you can think of this book as a parenting book in disguise. All of the lessons here can be used as strategies to help support a kid's creativity. (I hope you'll learn them for yourself first, so you can set a good example.)

At some point in your creative life, you might discover that, in the words of Murray Stein, you are your "own worst enemy, harshest critic, and severest taskmaster." You can lose touch with all that energy, joy, and freedom you felt when you were just starting out. Whether you've failed to achieve your goals or had success beyond your wildest dreams, it's easy to get bored, stuck, or find yourself just going through the motions. You feel washed-up. Burned-out. Like you'll never make anything good again.

Being around my kids liberated me from so many of these feelings. These are the lessons I learned. I hope they will help you.

"Every child is an artist. The problem is how to remain an artist once he grows up."

—PABLO PICASSO

① THROW OUT THE INSTRUCTIONS.

DON'T CALL IT ART.

When they were little, my kids were great at making art because they weren't worrying about making art.

Trying to make art is the easiest way to keep yourself from actually making art. When you're trying to make art, your head is full of all kinds of instructions about what is and isn't art and what you should and shouldn't do. But if you don't call it art, you take all the pressure off. Now you can just make stuff.

If you're not worried about making art, then you don't have to worry about any art critics. Little kids don't have a critic in their heads until we put one there. Once an inner critic takes up residence, we say all kinds of horrible things to ourselves that we would *never* say to others. Our inner art critic asks us who we think we are, what we think we're doing, where we get the nerve, why we even bother, when we are going to get serious and get a real job, how we expect to make a living, when we are going to do something *original*, and why we expect anyone to ever care about this absolute *crap* we are producing.

"Were we to meet this figure socially, this accusatory character, this internal critic, this unrelenting fault-finder, we would think there was something wrong with him," writes Adam Phillips. "He would just be boring and cruel. We might think that something terrible had happened to him, that he was living in the aftermath, in the fallout, of some catastrophe. And we would be right."

Luckily, art critics are only interested in art. If you don't call it art, the critics won't care what you're doing, and they'll leave you alone.

Now you can do whatever you want.

not

knowing is the first step

IT'S BETTER WHEN YOU DON'T KNOW.

"When you don't know what you're doing, you make some wonderful mistakes."

—PETER HOOK

In the beginning, we don't know enough to know that we don't know what we're doing. Kids don't know what can't be done until someone tells them they can't do it. The impossible is still possible.

In his book *The Element*, Sir Ken Robinson told a story about a six-year-old girl in a drawing lesson. Her teacher asked what she was drawing. "Without looking up, the girl said, 'I'm drawing a picture of God.' Surprised, the teacher said, 'But nobody knows what God looks like.' The girl said, 'They will in a minute.' "

This is the proper creative spirit—if only we could maintain it!

Trouble begins when someone tells us, or we discover on our own, that we don't know what we're doing. We start worrying whether what we're doing is any good and whether we're any good.

Many people stop at this point. The people who don't stop become artists.

When you don't know what you're doing but you've decided to do it anyway, you're willing to try anything. You fail a lot, but you occasionally stumble into brilliance. The filmmaker Orson Welles made his masterpiece *Citizen Kane* when he was twenty-five years old. Asked how he managed to make such an artful film at a young age, he emphasized the role of his ignorance. "I didn't know that there were things you couldn't do," Welles said. "It's only when you know something about a profession that you're timid or careful."

Welles and his crew did seemingly impossible things "simply by not knowing that they were impossible."

The trouble with this fertile mode of *not knowing* is that if you stick with it long enough, you start to know what you're doing. Other people notice that you know what you're doing and ask you to do more of it. Suddenly, you go from being *unknown* to *known*, or what we call "successful": the world thinks you know what you're doing and rewards you for it.

But *knowing* is very dangerous for the creative person. Because the minute you know what you are doing is the minute things start to get boring. You either start boring others or, more likely, you start boring yourself.

"The magic was in the first years,
when we didn't know what we were doing,
when we were willing to try anything."

—ALEX VAN HALEN

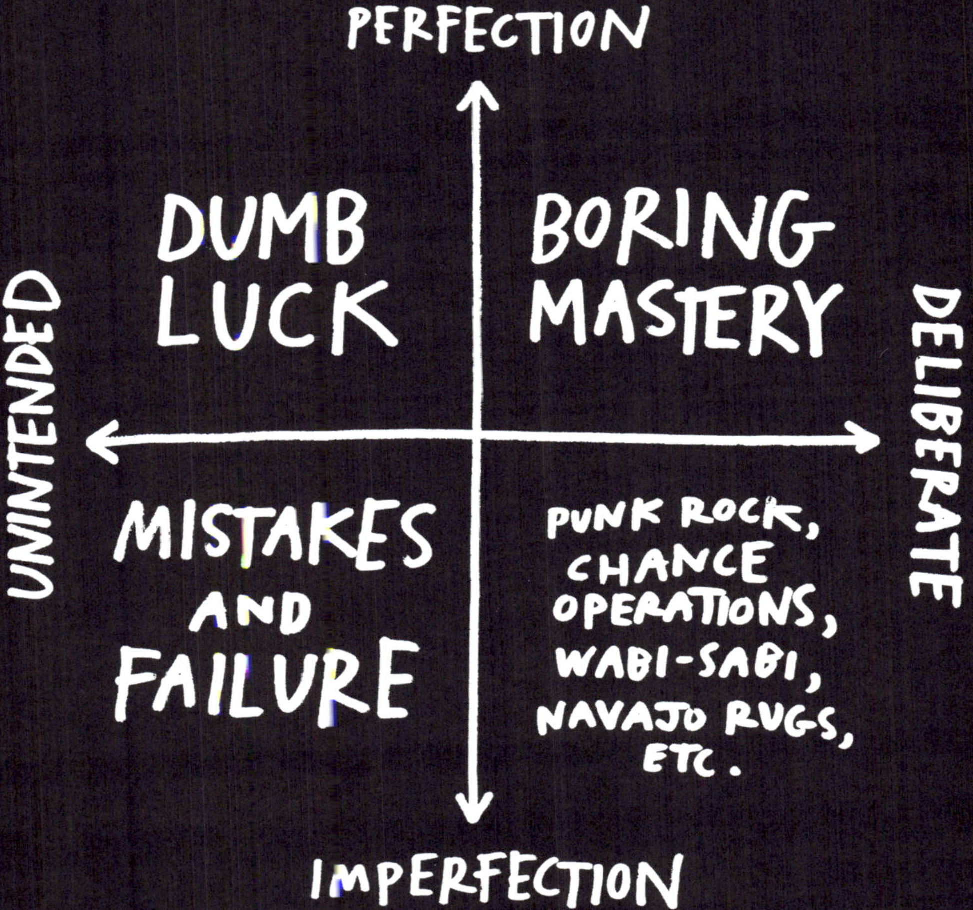

PERFECTION

UNINTENDED

DELIBERATE

DUMB LUCK

BORING MASTERY

MISTAKES AND FAILURE

PUNK ROCK, CHANCE OPERATIONS, WABI-SABI, NAVAJO RUGS, ETC.

IMPERFECTION

"I've heard people say that it takes 10,000 hours to master your style or your line or something," says the cartoonist Gareth Brookes, "but to be honest I think it takes 10,000 hours to become boring and mediocre. The moment you master something is the moment you stop being creative."

People who are able to stay creative their whole lives know that the minute they start knowing, it is time to go back to not knowing. They know that, as tempting as it is, if they remain in the safe, comfortable, and often lucrative mode of knowing, it will be nearly impossible to discover anything truly new.

As I write these words, one of the greatest rappers of our time is walking around playing a wooden flute. André Benjamin, aka André 3000, became wildly successful as one-half of the legendary hip-hop duo Outkast. But he turned away from rapping, saying no to millions of dollars and braving the disappointment of legions of fans in order to explore his love of wind instruments. His explanation? Mastery got *boring*. "I'd rather go amateur interesting than master boring," he said. When he first played the flute, he said it was like listening to himself "be a baby at something." It was an irresistible feeling. It was *not knowing*. (And what do you know—when he finally released his first album with wind instruments, it was nominated for three Grammy Awards.)

If you are currently in the *not knowing* mode—if the world doesn't make any sense right now and you have no idea what you're doing—you're in the right place! Stay there. Keep making stuff. See what happens.

"Don't think about making art, just get it done. Let everyone else decide whether it's good or bad, whether they love it or hate it. While they're deciding, make even more . . ."

—ANDY WARHOL

NOBODY KNOWS ANYTHING.

Some precocious children and wise teenagers get the sense that the adults around them only *pretend* to know what they're doing. They are exactly right.

The moment I held my firstborn, I realized just how much I didn't know. To be a parent is to be a perpetual amateur. In the original sense of the French word—"one who loves"—all you can do is show up and love the kid. The minute you think you have things figured out, the kid changes on you, and suddenly you have to try to figure things out all over again. This goes on for as long as the time you get together. If you get another kid to hang out with, you think, *Well, maybe what I learned with the last one will help with this one.*

who knows?

bank
on
not
knowing what's going to happen
or when,

don't think
long enough to know

not knowing
is
ok

Wrong! Turns out that every kid is different. So now you're winging it all over again.

In this way, being a parent is not unlike being an artist. You never get it figured out, and you never know for sure what you're doing. Your last project won't do your next one for you. What worked last time isn't guaranteed to work this time. This is true for all artists, even the great ones.

"Nobody knows anything," said the screenwriter William Goldman about Hollywood. "Not one person in the entire motion picture field knows for a certainty what's going to work. Every time out it's a guess—and, if you're lucky, an educated one."

As it is for Hollywood, so it is for all the arts, and the whole world, while we're at it. An individual human simply doesn't live long enough to know much of relatively anything. The writer Ernest Hemingway put it this way: "We are all apprentices in a craft where no one ever becomes a master."

The discovery that nobody knows anything can be frightening but also incredibly liberating, if you take it to heart. If nobody knows anything, you might have a shot at doing the things that you want to do after all. If nobody knows anything, you can figure things out on your own and do things your way. If nobody knows anything, nobody can tell you what to do.

"I can't remember any time in my life where I wasn't sitting looking at the grown-up scene . . . and thinking, This must be some great charade they've all agreed to play."

—DORIS LESSING

FIGURE IT OUT FOR YOURSELF.

I saw a sign on a playground once that read:

YOUR CHILDREN ARE FINE WITHOUT ADVICE OR SUGGESTIONS.

I suggest you make a copy of this sign and hang it wherever you do your creative work:

YOU ARE FINE WITHOUT ADVICE OR SUGGESTIONS.

We fill our heads with instructions of all kinds, always seeking out advice and suggestions from others. We buy books, attend courses, and read articles. We scroll social media for life hacks and tips from influencers. We compare our behind-the-scenes life to the crafted images our peers and strangers post online. If only we could just find the right instructions, we think, we could really know how to live.

But who can have any fun with a bunch of instructions in your head? It's like being a kid at the playground with a helicopter parent shouting at you to "Look out! Don't do that! Stop! Be careful! You're going to get hurt!" Or it's like buying one of those new branded LEGO sets, which are the equivalent of having kids build IKEA furniture. "Just follow the ninety-nine confusing steps we've laid out for you and you'll wind up with exactly what's on the box!"

Resist seeking out too much instruction from others. Try to figure things out on your own.

**"How to begin to educate a child.
First rule: leave him alone. Second rule: leave him alone.
Third rule: leave him alone. That is the whole beginning."**

—D. H. LAWRENCE

MESS
AROUND

FIND
OUT

What we learn on our own goes deeper and sticks with us longer than what we've been taught. The brilliant jazz pianist Bill Evans told his brother, Harry, that he could teach him in two minutes the musical tricks he was looking for, but Bill didn't want to deprive Harry of the pleasure of finding it out for himself. If you tell a student too much, Evans said, "you take his motivation away, because he hasn't discovered anything."

Besides, those who really seem to know what they're doing can't necessarily tell you how they do it. Paul McCartney, one of the greatest songwriters to ever live, is adamant that he does not know how songwriting works. In fact, that's the first thing he tells students when he is asked to teach: "I don't know how to do this. You would think I do, but it's not one of these things you ever know how to do."

Even the teachers who can tell you exactly what they know and what they're doing can't tell you exactly what *you* should do. No matter how good your teacher is, the learning must be done by you.

When we're forced to learn things on our own, we make our own discoveries. Decades before YouTube tutorials, the guitarist Adrian Belew taught himself to play guitar by listening to records.

Because he was unaware of all the studio trickery involved in many of his favorite recordings of guitarists like Jeff Beck or Jimi Hendrix, he found a way to reproduce the sounds without any effects pedals or fancy gear. From those experiments, he said he was "left with an urge to make the guitar sound like things it shouldn't be able to sound like." Belew would not necessarily be Belew if he had all the information at his fingertips that young musicians have today.

Our world is awash in information. What it's lacking is *wonder.* We think we need more information, when what we really need is to spend more time figuring things out on our own, fumbling about, exploring, getting lost, playing through our frustrations, and discovering something of our own.

"Every time we teach a child something, we keep him from inventing it himself."

—JEAN PIAGET

② DON'T
TAKE
THINGS
TOO
SERIOUSLY.

WHO'S HAVING FUN?

"The most mature human beings living are also childlike. That is not as contradictory as it sounds. The most mature people are the ones that can have the most fun."

—ABRAHAM MASLOW

Kids know how to have *fun.*

Remember fun?

I was reading an essay about the late Eve Babitz one time, and the writer wondered why she was having such a moment. I shouted to no one, "IT'S BECAUSE SHE WAS HAVING FUN—IN LIFE AND ON THE PAGE!"

It feels like barely anyone is having any fun right now and we need people to show us how it's done. When I'm out in the world these days, I'm not looking around for who's successful or who's doing great work; I'm looking for who seems to be having fun. When I identify such a person, I try to see if there's something I can steal from them.

"I am determined to have fun doing my work . . . if I'm enjoying myself then that feeling is passed on to the reader."

—ED EMBERLEY

The actor Jeff Bridges is someone who seems to have fun. When he was a kid and he was nervous about giving a performance, his mother called him over and said, "Remember: Have fun and don't take it too seriously!" Her words became his life philosophy—even when he was "at death's door" while undergoing treatment for cancer.

We're better at life when we're having fun and keeping things light. On the wall above my desk, I keep a framed picture of actor Bill Murray with a goofy look on his face and a Post-it note stuck to it that says "STAY LIGHT." The words came from a speech Murray gave a bunch of baseball players: "If you can stay light, and stay loose, and stay relaxed, you can play at the very highest level—as a baseball player or a human being."

Look around and ask yourself: "Who's having fun?"

It should be you.

“Ask yourself frequently, ‘Am I having fun?’ The answer needn’t always be yes. But if it’s always no, it’s time for a new project or a new career.”

—STEPHEN KING

PRETEND IT'S A COMEDY.

"One of the symptoms of approaching nervous breakdown is the belief that one's work is terribly important."

—BERTRAND RUSSELL

In 2020, during the early days of the pandemic, when my family was stuck in our tiny house together, the boys running wild and looking unkempt, there were times I felt like we were a bunch of shipwrecked castaways, floating aimlessly through our days. I picked up Dougal Robertson's memoir *Survive the Savage Sea.* It's a true story written by a dad who was literally stranded on a tiny dinghy with his family for thirty-seven days after a killer whale attack in the middle of the Pacific Ocean. I read the book to see if I could glean any dad-at-sea survival tips.

“If any single civilized factor in a castaway’s character helps survival,” Robertson wrote, “it is a well-developed sense of the ridiculous. It helps the castaways to laugh in the face of impossible situations and allows him, or her, to overcome the assassination of all civilized codes and characteristics which hitherto had been the guidelines of life.”

This wisdom rang true to my own experience. Even in a serious time of plague and death, the more I saw family life as a comedy, the better things seemed to go. The more we filled our house with merriment and laughter, the more we seemed to thrive.

“Even though it seems foolish and silly and crazy, comedy has the most to say about the human condition,” said the comedian Mel Brooks. “Because if you can laugh, you can get by. You can survive when things are bad if you have a sense of humor.”

When we think of life as a tragedy, we set ourselves up for failure. In his book *The Comedy of Survival*, Joseph Meeker argues

TRAGEDY	COMEDY
SPECIAL HERO	ORDINARY PERSON
TAKES ON THE WORLD	GETS INTO TROUBLE
BLOOD, SWEAT, TEARS	LAUGHTER, IMPROVISATION, WIT
SUCCESS IS THEIR UNDOING	FAILS OVER AND OVER
ENDS WITH DEATH (A FUNERAL)	ENDS WITH A BEGINNING (A WEDDING)

that all of Western civilization is built on the model of tragedy. Through great effort and much suffering, we have tried to shape the world in our image, with mostly catastrophic results. The only way to survive our disastrous times, Meeker proposes, is to start working under the model of comedy, playing and improvising our way through our lives, paying attention to what's actually in front of us, adapting to our circumstances, and making the most of what's available to us.

The story of creativity is often told as one of tragedy. Artist biographies are usually dramas of extraordinary people who suffer (and often die) for their work. They set out on a heroic mission against all odds, doing whatever it takes to make their vision a reality, leaving a trail of blood, sweat, and tears in their wake.

All stories become instructions for living: If you believe in art as tragedy, then in order to do creative work, you must be a genius or great talent, and you must suffer. You have to be willing to wreck your whole life and the lives of others just to make your art.

What would happen if we told the story as a comedy? In a comedy, ordinary people fumble about their lives, not knowing exactly what they're doing or where they're going. They get themselves into extraordinary situations. They fail a lot, but they remain playful and rely on their wits. They improvise and adapt. They make the most of things. They keep a sense of humor and stick around, because the ending of a comedy is always a happy one—every ending is the beginning of the rest of their lives.

That sounds like a story I want to be in.

Even when life is at its worst, it helps to pretend it's a comedy.

"Life itself is a comedy—a slap-stick comedy at that. It is always hitting you over the head with the unexpected. You reach to get the thing you want—slap! bang! It's gone! You strike at your enemy and hit a friend. You walk confidently, and fall. Whether it is tragedy or comedy depends on how you look at it. There is not a hair's breadth between them."

—CHARLIE CHAPLIN

COSMICOMIC PERSPECTIVE

JERRY SEINFELD PUT UP PICTURES FROM the HUBBLE SPACE TELESCOPE IN the *SEINFELD* WRITERS' ROOM. "IT WOULD CALM ME DOWN WHEN I WOULD START TO THINK THAT WHAT I WAS DOING WAS IMPORTANT," HE SAID.

AN ASTRONOMER'S WIFE HEARD THIS STORY AND TOLD ME HER HUSBAND DOES SOMETHING SIMILAR. "HE'LL SAY, 'IT'S JUST ASTRONOMY. WE'RE NOT SAVING LIVES HERE. IT'S OKAY IF WE FINISH TOMORROW INSTEAD OF TODAY...'"

PLAY THE FOOL.

Most of us spend a great deal of time and energy in our day-to-day lives trying our best not to look like a fool. My kids seemed to know from the minute they got here what a fool I was. I did nothing to dissuade them of their impression. We've had a lot of fun being fools together.

A fool's job is to run *fool's errands*. The fool's errands I ran with my kids—building sandcastles and sculptures out of driftwood on the beach, telling one another ridiculous stories and knock-knock jokes with bad punch lines, collaging fart balloons onto pictures of politicians we tore out of the newspaper, drawing in chalk all over the driveway, making an unrecordable racket in our music room jam sessions, stacking blocks into gigantic towers only to knock them down like Godzilla—all helped me get a little more foolish when I went out to the studio alone.

I didn't know the value of
nonsense.
And then one day, I'm
not
wearing
pants

What do I mean by a fool? "I don't mean a stupid, unthinking person," writes George Leonard in the epilogue of his book *Mastery*, "but one with the spirit of the medieval fool, the court jester, the carefree fool in the tarot deck who bears the awesome number zero, signifying the fertile void from which all creation springs, the state of emptiness that allows new things to come into being."

If you pull the card in a tarot deck, you'll see that The Fool is about to step off the edge of a cliff without a care in the world. The fool leaps before looking. The fool doesn't think too much. The fool just *does* stuff. The fool is optimistic that things will work out.

Like any good role, to play the fool wholeheartedly requires a not insignificant amount of courage.

"I think you have to kind of start with saying, 'I don't know. I don't know how the hell I'm going to do this at all,'" said the actor Philip Seymour Hoffman. "Really be as naive as possible, you know, as ignorant as possible, because then you can keep yourself as wide open as possible for anything that could be of help, could be of use."

To play the fool, start saying "I don't know," and keep saying it. "Whatever inspiration is," said the poet Wisława Szymborska, "it's born from a continuous 'I don't know.'"

Our fear of looking foolish holds us back from learning, trying new things, experimenting, and doing our most wild, daring, creative work. If you act as though you know everything, you will learn nothing and never discover anything new. It is much better to willingly play the fool.

"Children, in a very real sense, have beginners' minds, open to wider possibilities. They see the world with fresher eyes, are less burdened with preconception and past experience, and are less guided by what they know to be true. They are more likely to pick up details that adults might discard as irrelevant. Because they're less concerned with being wrong or looking foolish, children often ask questions that adults won't ask."

—TOM VANDERBILT

ASK A LOT OF QUESTIONS.

Kids ask a *lot* of questions. And the questions they ask can cut right to the heart of a matter and get straight to the mysteries of the universe. Even one question from a kid can flatten you. You're sitting there, minding your business, thinking you have a pretty good handle on things, and then a kid asks you, innocently, "If God made the universe, then who made God?"

Kids are naturally curious about the world and want to know more about it. Their open-mindedness, innocence, and naivety—the traits many adults see as their job to help kids grow out of—are exactly the things the most creative people manage to hold on to.

To really get to the root of things, you have to be willing to ask questions about the stuff that everyone except the young child takes for granted.

"An adolescent or an adult who writes poetry or does philosophy has to cultivate innocence to be able to puzzle and muse over the simplest ways we have of saying and seeing things," writes Gareth Matthews in *Philosophy and the Young Child*. "Sophistication may bring increased knowledge and, perhaps, a refined sensibility. But it may also encourage a cult of experts, dull sensitivity, and may reward flatulence in thought and language. Every society needs a barefoot Socrates to ask childishly simple (and childishly difficult!) questions, to force its members to reexamine what they have been thoughtlessly taking for granted."

The brightest scientists, artists, and other creative people value asking questions more than having all the answers. Sakichi Toyoda, the Japanese industrialist and founder of Toyota, developed a simple method to approach problems that could have been stolen from my own children: you simply ask a series of "Why?" questions five times in a row. (Anyone who's spent time with little kids knows that if they ask you "Why?" more than two or three times—

which they will!—the world suddenly becomes very strange and unknown to you.)

So, ask all the questions that pop into your head. Even questions that might seem silly can lead you to some of your most important work. The musician and filmmaker Matt Farley says the ridiculous idea that usually follows the beginning of the question "Wouldn't it be funny if . . ." is a great gift your brain has served up that you should pay attention to. If you reject such ideas, Farley says, "then the part of the brain that comes up with ideas is going to stop."

The questions you ask contain the clues for what you need to do next.

> **"The 'silly question' is the first intimation of some totally novel development."**
>
> **—ALFRED NORTH WHITEHEAD**

THE FIVE WHYS

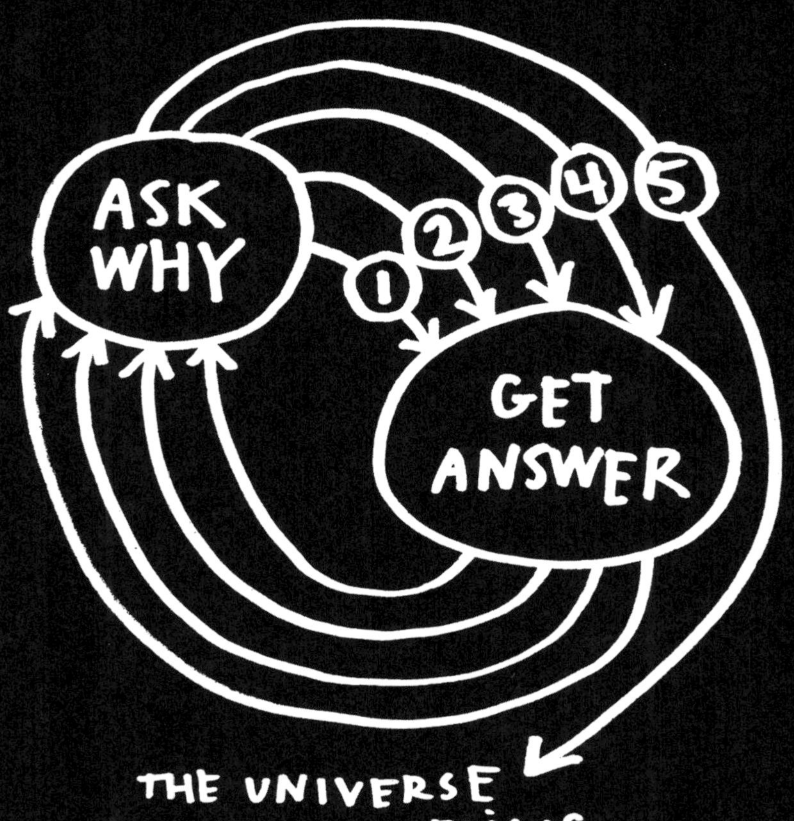

DON'T BE AFRAID TO DO WHAT COMES NATURALLY.

When he was little, my son Owen had the most beautiful handwriting and a gorgeous drawing line. But he had this funny way of holding a marker: he held it in his fist, with his thumb pointed down at the paper. It was never really a problem for him, but when we sent him to school, I was afraid he was going to wreck his wrist and that his teachers would fuss over his grip and want him to fix it. So, I showed him the "right way" to hold a pencil. That magic drawing line almost immediately disappeared. *Poof.*

This happens to us a lot in the creative life: We're getting along just fine, doing things in a way that comes naturally to us, and then somebody comes along and says we're doing it all wrong. Unfortunately, it's often the well-meaning people in our lives who are trying to help us who have the most power to really mess us up. It's much easier to ignore the mean people who we know really don't care about us.

Wanting what's best for ourselves, we often hobble our natural abilities by trying to *get serious* about our work and learn to do things the right way. After being accepted into the MFA program at Syracuse University, the writer George Saunders says he went up to his new mentor, Tobias Wolff, and assured him that he would no longer be writing "the silly humorous crap I applied to the program with, i.e., the stuff that had gotten me into the program in the first place." Now, Saunders said, he'd be doing "real writing."

"Well, good!" Wolff said. "Just don't lose the magic." Of course, Saunders says he immediately lost the magic, and it took him the entirety of grad school and several years after to get it back.

I see this pattern over and over with many creative people: they have this little bit of magic, a spark of something that comes

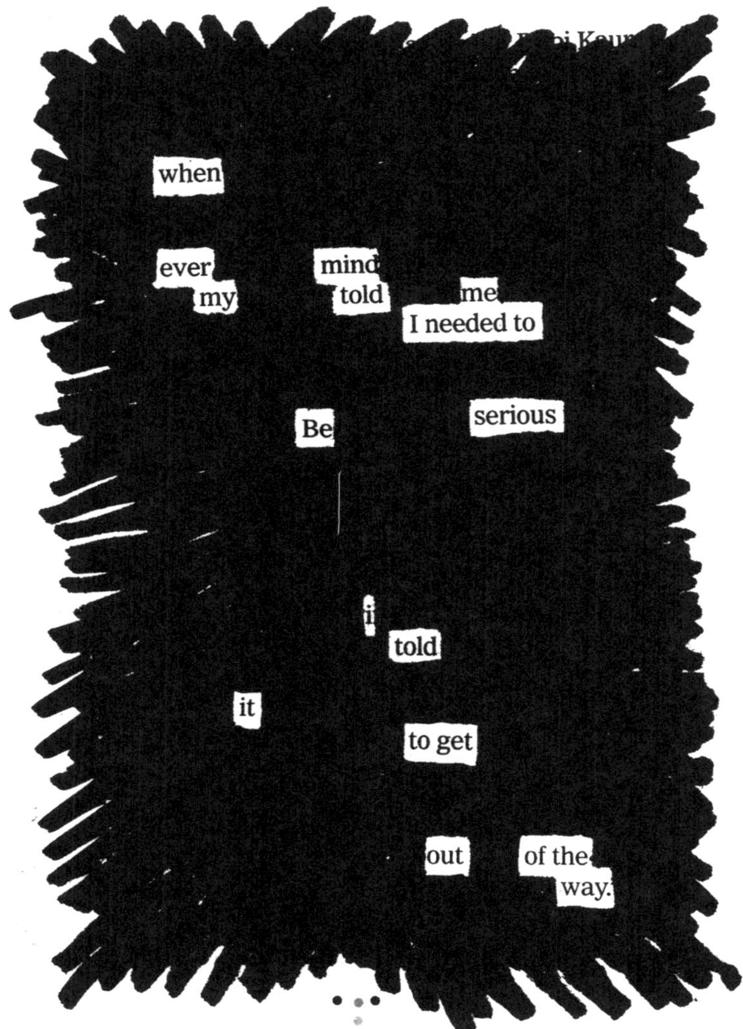
when
ever mind
my told me
I needed to
Be serious
i
told
it
to get
out of the
way.

naturally to them, and it's often messy and weird and a little bit off, and that's why they catch our attention in the first place. The odd magic is exactly what we love about them. Then, something happens. They decide, *Okay, people are watching me, it's time, now, to be serious*, and they go off and lose their magic.

Don't let this happen to you! Don't be afraid to do what comes naturally. Fight the urge to do things the "right" way. Don't lose the magic.

"I think children are also the most brilliant artists, don't you? There's nothing more perfect than a child's drawings. In order to create work, I often have to try and reach back to that open-mindedness, I suppose, and the naïveté that children have. Things pour out of them in such a natural way. I keep trying to get closer to that."

—PJ HARVEY

③ GIVE YOURSELF TIME, SPACE, AND MATERIALS.

MAKE A SPACE

FILL IT WITH MATERIALS

FIND TIME TO GO THERE

"The elements of time, space, and materials make it possible for children to explore, invent, and make their ideas visible. It's the combination of unhurried and uninterrupted time, inviting spaces, and materials that guide mind and hands, that invite creative thinking."

—URSULA KOLBE

Play is the work of the child and the artist. Artists and children both need the right combination of time, space, and materials. Time is best when it's unhurried and uninterrupted. Space should be inviting, inspiring, and comfortable. Materials should be plentiful and at hand.

Creative play can proceed when all these elements are available, but if any of these elements are missing, you can run into trouble. If you give yourself time and space but no materials, you have nothing to play with. If you give yourself time and materials but no space, you have nowhere to play. If you give yourself space and materials but no time, your play cannot even begin.

If you run into trouble, you can try to get out of it by tweaking these three elements. Try working at a different time of day or for a different length of time. Find a new space or rearrange your old one. Go out and find yourself some new materials or pull out some old supplies you haven't used in a while.

Sometimes you can make up for a lack of one element by boosting the others. If you don't have a dedicated space, for example, you can create a portable studio of materials that you can bring with you anywhere. If you have limited time, you can create a space filled with materials that can be constantly ready for you. If you have no materials, you can go out and find some.

Let's explore these elements one by one.

<u>The Rules of the Studio</u>

1. No yelling
2. No fighting
3. .No food or drink
   (except for water
   or papa's coffee)
4. If you need help ask
   for it!
5. If it's not fun,
   work on something
   else!!!!

TIME TO TRAVEL IN

My parents worked a lot, so they gave me the great gift of being home alone with lots of free time. I wanted to give my kids the same gift, because it was in all that free time that I learned to time travel.

We all travel through time to a certain extent, but the artist travels *out* of it. When an artist is fully immersed in their play, they are not so much "in the moment" as they are *out of time* completely. The psychologist Mihaly Csikszentmihalyi called this state "flow." Others call it being "in the zone." In many ways, it is the best thing the creative life has to offer us, the state so many of us chase when we go into the studio. In this state, you forget time even exists. "To be out of time, to be in that other state," said the poet Anne Carson, "is completely fun." It's playtime.

The trouble is: in order to forget about time, you have to spend a lot of time thinking about time and working with time. You have to schedule time in order to get out of it.

I schedule playtime for myself. On a regular basis, I block out chunks on my calendar with a start and finish time that are reserved exclusively for play. During these times, nothing is required of me other than being in my studio and messing around.

This might not sound like serious business. Adults tend to undervalue play because we see it as the opposite of work. But this is totally wrong. "The opposite of play is not work," wrote the play researcher Stuart Brown. "The opposite of play is depression."

If you haven't played lately, you probably need playtime more than you think you do. Brown says that when we deny our playful selves, we develop a "play deficit" that is much like a sleep deficit—it takes a while to catch back up. "When play is denied over the long term, our mood darkens." The more you deny your playful self, the more chance you have of breaking down, burning out, and just generally being a miserable human being.

If you still feel the need to justify playtime for yourself, consider it part of your research and development budget. Because playtime is all about tinkering, puttering around, and experimenting without worrying about productivity, it's paradoxically the time you're most likely to stumble upon something you can really use in your work.

When I take a day "off," I tell myself I'm not going to do any work, I'm just going to poke into the studio and play around a bit. On those days I often wind up getting much more done than when I force myself to "work"—I'll make a bunch of collages or poems just for the heck of it or come up with a great idea while doodling in my notebook. On the best days, I look up and I'm already out of time.

> **"What did you do as a child that made the hours pass like minutes? Herein lies the key to your earthly pursuits."**
>
> **—CARL JUNG**

~~PLAY IT SAFE~~

MAKE IT SAFE TO PLAY

A SAFE SPACE TO PLAY

I always had a playroom when I was growing up, but after my parents divorced, my mom basically gave me my own half of our ranch house. Technically, I've never had a studio with more square footage! I had enough room for an old church piano, a full drum set, all sorts of instruments and recording equipment, a drawing desk, books, a computer, a stereo, a couch, and a TV. My friends would come over and we'd jam for hours, making an ungodly racket and getting up to all sorts of creative mischief. My mom says she never minded the noise because she knew where I was. It was a safe space to play.

It was also a safe place to *hide*. Creative kids thrive when they have a good hiding spot—a bedroom, a basement, a tree house—some place where they can get away from the world (and their parents) and safely enter a world of their own.

I wanted to make sure I gave my kids the same kind of space I had, even though they've grown up in a house much smaller than the one I grew up in. Where there's a will, there's a way: When the musician Iggy Pop was growing up in a trailer park, his parents gave him their bedroom in the trailer because it was the only room big enough to fit his drum set. Talk about room to play!

An artist needs *room*. Not a whole room, necessarily, but *room*. Room for the artist can be made in the home or outside of the home. Most artists dream of a whole structure apart from their living space—a studio in a big building, a shed, or even a garage. They're lucky to get a basement, an attic, or their own bedroom. Sometimes the artist must settle for a desk in the corner or the kitchen table.

"The studio is a safe space for stupidity."

—WILLIAM KENTRIDGE

AN UNSTAGED PHOTO OF A REAL SCENE I STUMBLED UPON IN OUR BATHROOM ↲

FIND A GOOD HIDING SPOT.

The space available will constrain, to some extent, the qualities of the artist's play. A kitchen table can handle a sketchbook and watercolors, but maybe not an easel and oil paints. A bedroom wall can absorb an acoustic guitar, but maybe not heavy metal drumming. Real estate is a real constraint. As the musician Ian Svenonius joked, "Once upon a time, a group called the Clash sang, 'We're a garage band.' But who can afford a garage nowadays?"

It helps to have a space where you can really make a mess, leave it, and come back to it tomorrow. "At my son's school, if he was doing something creative and had to transition to another project, they would put a work-save card on it and say just don't touch it," said the artist and actress Lucy Liu. "And that's essentially what a studio is. The whole space is a work-save card."

"You have to create a safe place, where you can play. This involves first creating boundaries of space, and then boundaries of time."

—JOHN CLEESE

It also helps to have a space that's *private*. If you want to be your wildest, most creative self, you need to be able to hide from the world and remove yourself from the surveillance of other human beings.

If your work is portable, or you can make it so, sometimes you can find room to play out in the world, in what Ray Oldenburg called "third places," such as parks, libraries, or cafés. (Your "first place" is home, your "second place" is work.) Many of these third places are disappearing from modern life, but you may be able to find them in unexpected locations.

You might even discover that working out in the world is better than working in your own space. My favorite example of this is the novelist Amy Daws, who found the cure for writer's block at her local tire shop. After bringing her car in for new tires and getting a bunch of writing done, she started taking her friends' cars in for maintenance work so she had an excuse to write there. Eventually, the management of the tire shop just invited her to come hang out whenever she wanted to.

Sometimes when you work out in the world you can find something you can bring home with you. John Swartzwelder wrote much of his great material for *The Simpsons* in a diner while smoking and drinking tons of coffee. He discovered what I've discovered: there's something magical about being tucked into a diner booth. When California banned smoking in public places, he decided to buy a diner booth of his own and install it in his house so he could keep working the way he liked to.

There's something about unassuming spaces that relaxes us. Many creative people I admire have done their work in fast-food restaurants. My friend Jason Polan liked to draw at Taco Bell. A young David Sedaris wrote on the back of place mats at IHOP. The film director David Lynch was notorious for hanging out at Bob's Big Boy.

"I used to go to Bob's Big Boy restaurant just about every day from the mid-seventies until the early eighties," Lynch writes in *Catching the Big Fish*. "I'd have a milk shake and sit and think. There's a safety in thinking in a diner. You can have your coffee or your milk shake, and you can go off into strange dark areas, and always come back to the safety of the diner."

This is the best kind of space to give yourself: a safe zone in which you can wander off and come back.

IN-N-OUT

MATERIALS AT HAND

"I asked my mother, what should I teach my kids?
She said don't teach them anything,
just give them lots of supplies."

—TONY MILLIONAIRE

Kids need lots of things to play with. So do artists.

The things we give ourselves to play with shape the kinds of ideas we have. You might think that art is a one-way street in which an artist has ideas and then finds the proper materials to bring those ideas to life. But I've found that just as often, it is playing with materials that brings forth the ideas.

Materials can be cheap and crude or they can be expensive and sophisticated. If you can get your hands on the finest materials you can afford, that's wonderful, but it is worth remembering what we learn from toddlers at play: you can give them all the fancy toys you want, but nothing really beats a good stick, some string, a cardboard tube, water, dirt, or rocks. Many a parent has known a Christmas morning where the box the toy came in gets played with more than the toy itself. (A toy rocket is a toy rocket, but a box can be anything.)

Our materials should be playthings. Finding your material might take some trial and error. The artist Anni Albers thought that artists come to their material *accidentally*. "Something speaks to us, a sound, a touch, hardness or softness, it catches us and asks us to be formed." You'll know when you find your material, because it will speak to you. It will invite you to play.

We need tools to do work, but we need *toys* to really be at play. Your tools should feel like toys that you can play with.

When the classical pianist Phyllis Chen got tendinitis in both arms, she found playing on a toy piano less painful than playing on a grand piano. She also discovered that the toy piano liberated her from the seriousness and stifling tradition of the grand piano. The toy piano took the pressure off with "a childlike feeling of finding the loophole." She even started writing her own music for the first time. When she returned to playing a regular piano, she had a fresh way of approaching it. Chen learned something about toys that I learned from my kids: if you put an old toy away for a while and then bring it back, it becomes a new toy.

Nothing makes us want to play like a new toy. Put your old toys away and start playing with some new ones. If you can't seem to write good songs on your trusty guitar, pick up a mandolin and start noodling around. (That's how Peter Buck wrote the riff for R.E.M.'s biggest hit, "Losing My Religion.") Once you forget what it's like to hold a guitar, you can pick it up again and it'll feel new.

TOYS GET MORE INTERESTING WHEN WE CAN LOOK INSIDE AND SEE HOW THEY WORK.

Different tools and materials want to do different things. Pen on paper wants to do one thing, and oil paint on canvas wants to do something else. Pressing piano keys gives us different ideas than strumming the strings of a guitar. Cardboard and glue can take us places that a wheel and clay don't want to go. In order to have the widest variety of ideas, we should fill our spaces with the widest variety of materials we can get our hands on, play with them, and see what happens.

The picture book creator Jon Klassen points out that when you learn to think about your material in this playful way, you discover that you yourself are a material. You find out what you are made of and what you really want to create.

“Being creative is not so much the desire to do something as the listening to that which wants to be done: the dictation of the materials.”

—ANNI ALBERS

④ PERMISSION TO BE BAD!

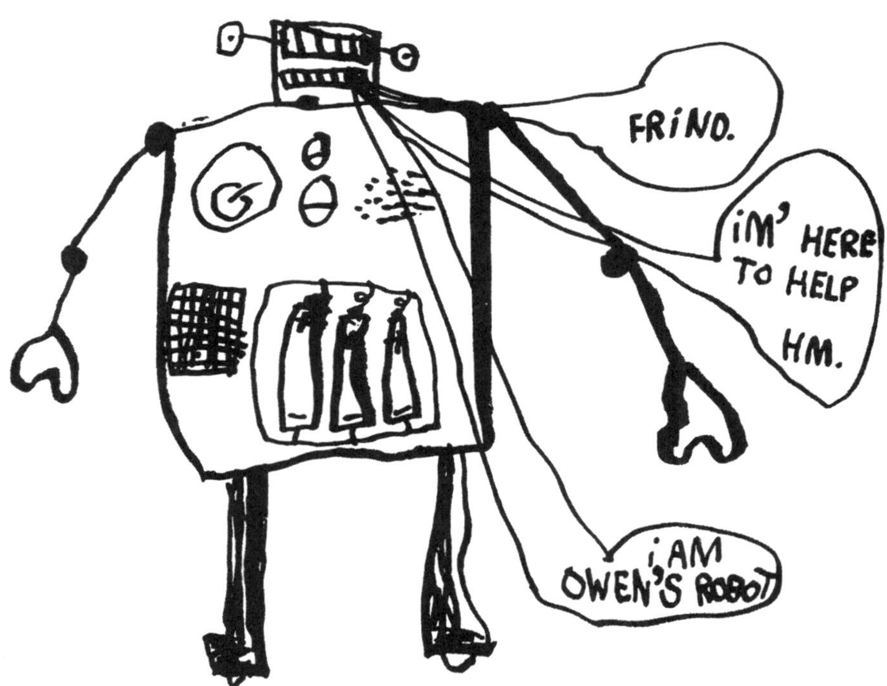
FRiND.
iM' HERE TO HELP HM.
i AM OWEN'S ROBOT

DO SOMETHING YOU SHOULDN'T.

"Artists must be allowed to go through bad periods! They must be allowed to do bad work! They must be allowed to get in a mess! They must be allowed to have dud experiments! They must also be allowed to have periods where they repeat themselves in a rather aimless, fruitless way before they can pick up and go on."

—DAVID SYLVESTER

My kids seem to be at their most creative when they're really supposed to be doing something else. Sometimes I feel like I spend all day telling strangers, "Start reading! Start drawing! Start making music!" and then I spend all evening telling my kids to "Stop reading! Stop drawing! Stop making music! Brush your teeth and go to bed!"

There's something about *mischief*—goofing off, getting into trouble, dodging responsibilities—that seems to activate the creative spirit. Some of the most creative stuff I saw during the stay-at-home era of the pandemic was the catalogue of ways students found of getting out of their virtual schoolwork, like using a Google Doc on their Chromebooks as a chat room or a looped video of themselves looking engaged as their Zoom screen.

It's fun to be like those kids, if only temporarily: to set aside our serious work, to be a little naughty, and to do what we're not supposed to do.

"I always make sure that when I go into the studio I do something that I feel like doing," writes the artist Nick Bantock, "and not something I should or ought to do. Even if it's only for the first twenty minutes, it's important to be obligation free."

i like the

GOOD

that is obtained from

trying to

not

be

GOOD

I would go even further: you should start your day doing something you think you *shouldn't* be doing.

Close your eyes and think of the most uptight authority figure in your life. (It might be you!) Now make a list of all the things you could make that would disappoint or horrify this person. Pick something on the list, set a timer for twenty minutes, and try to make that thing.

Do the most *unserious* things you can think of. Do what sounds totally stupid and wrong. Do what sounds fun.

If you can't come up with your own list, do the kinds of things I did as a bored, sulky, high school student trying to fill time: Doodle band logos all over a page in your notebook. Cut a bunch of pictures out of a magazine and glue them to a piece of notebook paper. Turn up the most embarrassing music you can think of to the loudest volume you can stand and play air guitar in front of a mirror.

See how it makes you feel, and whether you could bring some of that feeling into your work for the rest of the day.

I think you'll discover what kids already know: It's no fun trying to *be good*. It's more fun to *be bad*.

MAKE A BIG PILE OF IMPERFECT THINGS.

At the age of four, my son Jules drew like nobody I'd ever seen. He attacked the page with full confidence, exclaiming to himself, often pumping his fists in excitement over a mark he'd made. If he messed up a drawing, he'd throw it on the floor and start a new one. If he finished a perfect drawing, he'd throw it on the floor and start a new one. It wasn't about the drawings; it was all about the *drawing.*

Throughout the day, Jules's drawings would pile up on the floor. Every night, we'd sweep them up with a big broom, pluck out any we couldn't stand to lose, and put the rest in the recycle bin. Then we'd make sure to refresh the markers and paper supply. Jules would often blow through a single package of printer paper in a few days. We never said a word to him about wasting materials.

In his memoir, *Chuck Amuck*, the animator Chuck Jones said there was a silver lining to his father's repeated failures in business: every time one of his father's companies folded, he gave all the kids "acres of the finest Hammermill bond stationery" and "hundreds of boxes of pencils" emblazoned with the doomed company's name. "We were forbidden—actually forbidden—to draw on both sides of the paper."

Jones said that together his parents created a near-perfect environment for art-making: "the opportunity to draw, free from excessive criticism, and free from excessive praise—Mother, because she felt that children in the exploration of life could do no wrong, and Father . . . because he only wanted to get rid of that paper as soon as possible."

When you're not worried about wasting your precious supplies, you don't have to worry about being perfect.

Perfectionism is something to be battled at every stage of the artist's life. Perfectionism is the impossible, imaginary standard in our heads that we will never live up to. It's better to embrace *imperfectionism*—to make a mess, to court accidents and mistakes, to actively set ourselves up for failure, to fail early, and to fail often.

One way to do this is to worry about the *quantity* of what you produce instead of the *quality*.

In the book *Art & Fear*, David Bayles and Ted Orland tell a parable about a ceramics teacher who split his students into two groups. "All those on the left side of the studio, he said, would be graded solely on the quantity of the work they produced, all those on the right solely on its quality." The teacher graded the quantity group by the pounds of pottery they produced, and the quality group by the one "perfect" pot they created. "The works of highest quality were all produced by the group being graded for quantity," Bayles and Orland wrote. "It seems that while the 'quantity' group was busily churning out piles of work—and learning from their mistakes—the 'quality' group had sat theorizing about perfection, and in the end had little more to show for their efforts."

MY FRIEND DREW DERNAVICH'S PILES OF CARTOONS SUBMITTED TO THE NEW YORKER

This parable speaks to my own experience: if I sit down to make one perfect poem, I usually get a stiff, crappy poem that I will throw out, but if I sit down and try to make a big stack of poems, I'll usually find at least one decent stanza in the stack.

"The finished pieces that we share—they're dependent on these messy piles of imperfection," said the cartoonist Sarah Leavitt in a talk to students. "What if you make a big pile of imperfect things? What if your job is experimentation, exploring, repeating, failing, learning, continuing?" To foster this spirit in the classroom, Leavitt actively encourages her students to waste paper! "You will not be the reason that our forests disappear," she jokes.

So don't fret over wasting your materials. Don't hoard art supplies for "important" projects. Use up everything you've got on whatever you're working on. Wasting materials is all part of the process: either learn to be okay with waste or only give yourself materials you're okay seeing wasted.

Make a big pile of imperfect things. Eventually, something in the pile might be worth saving.

5
BELIEVE
IN
MAGIC.

DRESS-UP AND SILLY RITUALS

Playing with my kids taught me that the creative spirit is not just something you possess; it's something you *inhabit*. Entering the creative spirit is about more than just going within; it's about stepping into something that's outside of you.

In his book *Homo Ludens*, the Dutch historian Johan Huizinga wrote about a "magic circle" of time and space that all creative play takes place within. The magic circle is like a portal that transports us to a temporary world—a virtual playground in which the rules of ordinary life do not apply.

Artists are like kids: for them, there is a very fine line between the imaginary world and the real world. The veil between the immaterial and the material stays razor-thin. The artist crosses back and forth between these worlds, and the problems they face are ones of entry and reentry—getting out of the world and into the spirit, and then having to get out of the spirit and ease back into the world. These transitions can be bumpy, if not painful.

You can establish rituals to help ease these transitions. The sillier the rituals the better, because silliness helps us get into the spirit of play. Our silly rituals draw magic circles that we can step into. They are portals that help us enter into our playful selves.

I do all kinds of silly stuff in the studio. I buy pencils that look like fake cigarettes at the toy store down the street and dangle them from my lips and "smoke" while I'm writing. When I start a new notebook, I weigh it on a postage scale, and when I finish it, I weigh it again to see how much weight it gained. While writing this book, I found an old knit cap I used to wear in high school and dubbed it my "thinking cap," putting it on before I wrote.

Try playing dress-up! A costume is a powerful device: When you put on an apron, a jumpsuit, or some special item of clothing, your body feels the material and tells your brain that it's playtime. When it's time to play, put on your costume. When it's time to stop, take it off.

Masks are a particular kind of costume. They allow us to be things we can't be in everyday life. Masks can be literal or metaphorical. A pseudonym is a mask that the writer puts on so they can be another person. Prince had so much music in him that his record company couldn't release it all—so he invented other groups that he could write for, channeling different parts of his personality into alter egos. The rapper Daniel Dumile, aka MF DOOM, put on a literal and metaphorical mask—he never went onstage without his "metalface," and his various alter egos allowed him to explore the darker sides of himself while leading a normal, anonymous life.

An actor uses props to get into character. So can you. Collect talismanic items to keep around you when you're working—a lucky

> **"I believe that magic is art and that art—whether it be writing, music, sculpture, or any other form—is literally magic."**
>
> **—ALAN MOORE**

PUT ON A MASK SO YOU CAN TELL THE TRUTH.

toy or a special object with meaning. I heard from a reader once who told me he uses some of the art supplies he inherited from his grandfather, and this helps him feel close to his grandfather, like he's in the room. I sometimes feel when I'm drawing that the ghost of a passed-on friend is haunting my brush.

I like to get a little spooky in the studio. Spooky is a cousin to silly—they're both about getting outside of your normal self. I'm a book nerd, so I like to practice *bibliomancy*—receiving messages about what to do next by randomly choosing a passage from a book. I keep a paper dictionary in my studio just for this purpose. When I don't know what to write about, I'll flip to a random page, close my eyes, point my finger, open my eyes, and read the entry my finger is pointing to. When his band was looking for a name, lead singer Michael Stipe flipped to a random page of the dictionary and found R.E.M.

Whatever works. It's all about getting into the spirit. Come up with your own silly rituals, or steal a few from other artists, if they've had the guts to tell us about them. Here's one I like but haven't tried yet: Whenever the picture book author Ed Emberley needed to clear his head, he'd lie down on the couch and say "baloney sandwich" three times. Give it a try!

MESSAGES FROM THE UNIVERSE

"The universe is full of magical things patiently waiting for our wits to grow sharper."

—EDEN PHILLPOTTS

Young children believe in magic until they grow up or get talked out of it. For the very young child, almost everything is *alive*, and children ascribe feelings and thoughts to all sorts of inanimate objects. When the world is enchanted and full of magic, it is very easy to find rich meaning in everything, to play, to make things up, and to pretend.

OVERHEARD WORDS I STOLE FROM A KID →

DON'T LET YOUR DREAMS GIVE UP ON YOU

When my kids were very little, they would say the most magical, poetic things on a daily basis. I wrote some of them down. While we were walking around the city at nighttime: "Look, Papa, the moon is following us." Sitting around the flames of a campfire: "The fire looks like it's trying to tell us a story." Going inside the house after hearing thunder: "God sends a storm when he feels like being alone."

Children find magic everywhere because they believe in it, and the artist who believes in magic will find it, too. The writer Henry Miller thought that the artist was simply a person who has antennae, "who knows how to hook up to the currents which are in the atmosphere." You must learn to put up your antennae, to be ready to receive messages from the universe, to read its signs, and to take dictation from the unsayable.

Where do ideas come from, anyway? Just as it helps to think of the creative spirit as something we enter into, it also helps to think of ideas as things that visit us, rather than things we have. Musicians and songwriters are particularly good at this kind of magical thinking. Ideas, says Nick Cave, "are not inside you, unable to get out; rather, they are outside of you, unable to get in."

You must make yourself ready to receive ideas. If you aren't ready to receive the ideas, the ideas might go visit someone else. This might sound delusional to the rational, adult mind, but it's the kind of magical thinking that works. "If you're going to live your life based on delusions (and you are, because we all do)," writes Elizabeth Gilbert in *Big Magic*, "then why not at least select a delusion that is helpful?"

One way to boost your curiosity about the world is to assume that everything in life is a clue left from the universe for you to investigate. In this magical mode of operating, you find meaning in randomness and chance, and there's no such thing as a coincidence.

Take everything as a sign and you'll be less stumped about what to do next.

"Children are mystical-minded creatures; they sense the strangeness of it all. As we settle into earthly life, this sense fades."

—JANET MALCOLM

Quiet, Friends:

I am Listening for

Another

World

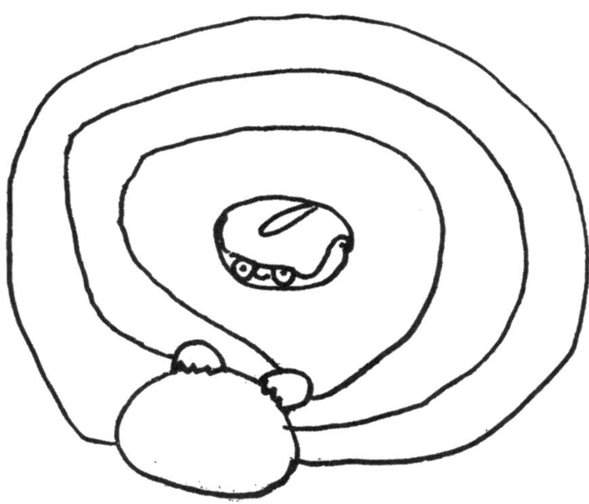

⑥ THINK OUTSIDE YOUR HEAD.

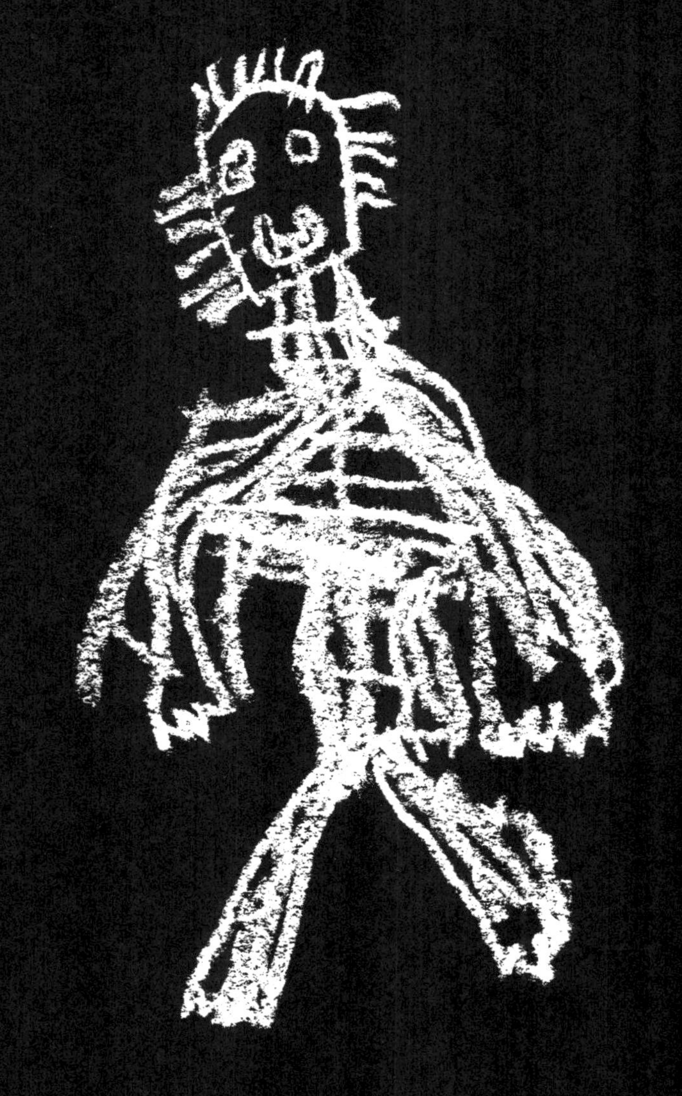

"I don't really think the artist is an intellectual. I believe that the artist is a set of nerves."

—WAYNE WHITE

Children learn and think with their whole bodies. Babies crawl everywhere and put everything in their mouths. Toddlers shout and climb and dance and swing and run around and have to touch everything. Little kids learn by poking and prodding the world, mimicking the people around them, and asking a lot of questions.

When we grow up, we think learning and thinking happens in our heads. If we drew a picture of someone thinking, we'd probably copy Rodin's sculpture, *The Thinker*: a lone individual, sitting still, pondering deeply, unbothered, and without distraction. In her book *The Extended Mind*, Annie Murphy Paul calls this "brainbound" thinking. Her message is one that almost all creative people discover eventually: like children, we do some of our best thinking *outside our heads*.

Getting into the creative spirit is a whole-body exercise. Where does the dancer, for example, do most of their thinking—in their head or with their feet? When a cartoonist is drawing, the hand tells the brain as much as the brain tells the hand. The feel of the clay tells the potter how to proceed. An artist is like an octopus with multiple brains in their appendages—their "main brain" is telling them one thing, but their other brains are talking back at them.

Artists learn to go on their nerve. When the producer Quincy Jones described being in the studio making some of his classic albums, he said, "We simply did what gave us the goosebumps." The writer Vladimir Nabokov suggested that we should read books not with our brains, but with our *spines*. He said that the best reading had to offer is "that little shiver" or "tingle" that runs through us when we read something good. Whenever the writer Leonard Shlain made a great connection in his work, he could almost feel his scalp tingle. "To me," he wrote, "setting my scalp atingle is one of the most enjoyable aspects of writing."

You can feel it in your body when you're doing something right.

Learn to trust your sensations—the gut feelings, the goose bumps, the hairs standing on the back of your neck—those are symptoms of your body knowing things before your brain does.

I once clipped out a newspaper article called "How to Draw Blood." A nurse described having to "develop intelligence in your fingers." Her point was that every vein in every arm is different, and not only do you have to *think* when you draw blood, but you also have to *feel* your way through the procedure. I crossed out the word "blood" in the clipping, because what she learned about drawing blood was exactly what I'd learned about drawing with a pencil.

There's great intelligence in your body if you can learn how to use it.

Think outside your head.

> **"The great thing in all education is to make our nervous system our ally instead of our enemy."**
>
> **—WILLIAM JAMES**

LISTEN TO YOUR BODY.

When our babies were crying, we learned a triage checklist from the parenting book *The Happiest Baby on the Block*:

Is the baby hungry? Is the baby tired? Is their diaper wet?

I started using this checklist on myself when I was in the studio:

Are you hungry? Are you tired? Do you need a change?

Because so much creative thinking happens in our bodies, it's hard to do much of it when our bodies are too out of whack. A lot of what ails us could be cured with a sandwich, a nap, or a hot bath.

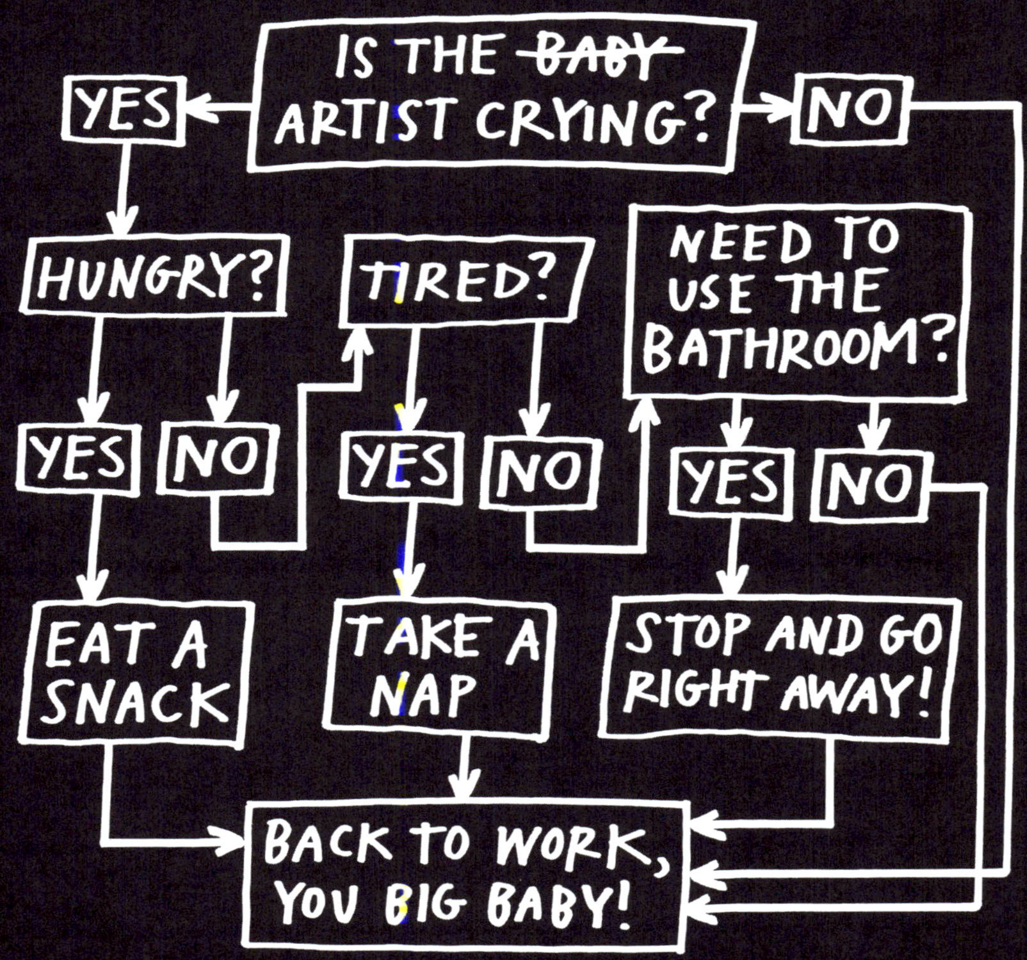
IS THE ~~BABY~~ ARTIST CRYING?
YES
NO
HUNGRY?
TIRED?
NEED TO USE THE BATHROOM?
YES
NO
YES
NO
YES
NO
EAT A SNACK
TAKE A NAP
STOP AND GO RIGHT AWAY!
BACK TO WORK, YOU BIG BABY!

Hunger is the easiest to deal with. Feed yourself! Fetch a snack. Keep your favorite treats around for when you get peckish. (The Beatles never entered the recording studio without tea and biscuits.) Make sure you're drinking enough water. Take yourself out to lunch. Cook yourself a meal. (If your hunger is of an intellectual or inspirational kind, skip ahead to the next chapter.)

Fatigue is easily dealt with as well. Lie down for a quick nap! Establish a good sleep schedule and try to stick to it. Take notice of your natural rhythms—are you an early bird or a night owl? Build a daily routine that suits you.

Rest is an important part of the creative process. Be sure to take a weekly Sabbath of some kind. You need a day off when you rest and relax and don't do anything related to art-making. I find that if I spend one single day away from the studio it's enough to get me itching to return.

As for a change, it might be as simple as going to the bathroom. But it's possible you need another change of some kind.

Take a break. Call a friend. Clean up your desk. Fiddle around. (I like to keep a Rubik's Cube on my desk for when I get bored.)

Get your body moving. Annie Murphy Paul points out the words we use when we're uninspired—we get "stuck" or "in a rut"—and the words we use when things are going well—we're "on a roll" or our thoughts are "flowing." Put on a song and dance around. Stretch. Do some push-ups. Get your wiggles out!

If you're feeling claustrophobic, flee to the outdoors. Spend some time in nature. "Listen to the birds," Captain Beefheart counseled. "That's where all music comes from."

Go for a good long walk. "I'm not saying going for a walk will solve all your problems," wrote my friend, the writer Ryan Holiday. "I'm just saying there's no problem that's going to be made worse by going for a walk." When a walk won't cut it, I like to go for a bike ride. Catching one downhill coast can fix my whole day.

Another old parenting tip: "Just add water." If things get too dire, run a hot shower or take a nice warm bath or just wash the dishes. Soaking is good for the soul.

WORK WITH YOUR FEELINGS.

Kids feel all the big feelings. That's a good thing. Feelings are symptoms that show you're really alive in the world.

The trouble is what to do with your feelings. Everybody has big feelings, but artists are lucky, because they have something they can do with them. All the artist has to do is feel their feelings and find a way to channel those feelings into their work.

There's no need to go around trying to be a happy-go-lucky person. Let's face it: Many of us are drawn to creative work because we are maladjusted! If you thought the world was perfect, why would you bother adding to it?

I have found some of my best work in my most negative emotions. Anger, for example, is dirty fuel, but it burns hot. This is the major message of punk rock: anger is an energy—you can use it.

"I am angry and curious," says the musician Henry Rollins. "These two things propel me forward."

The monk and peace activist Thich Nhat Hanh, or "Mr. Calm himself, Mr. Peace," as the writer bell hooks described him, once told her to hold on to her anger and use it as compost in her garden. "If we think of anger as compost, we think of it as energy that can be recycled in the direction of our good."

I have to be a little agitated to really get to work. I laughed in self-recognition when I read this description of the talk show host Regis Philbin by the coauthor of his memoirs, Bill Zehme: "Aggravation is an art form in his hands. Annoyance stokes him, sends him forth, gives him purpose. Ruffled, he becomes electric, full of play and possibility."

Disgust is also extremely helpful information. Whatever disgusts us in what other people are making, we can turn it around and do the opposite.

"I keep thinking that I shall have no more to say," said philosopher Mary Midgley, "and then finding some wonderfully

THINGS IM
AFRAID OF:
1. SPIDERS
2. MONTSERS
3. SKELATONS
4. FRANKNSTIN
5. DRAGELA
6. MUMMYS
SOMBIES
8. WITCHS

idiotic doctrine which I can contradict." She admitted it was "a negative approach, as they say, but one that doesn't seem to run out."

Some emotions just come with the creative territory. Fear and doubt, for example, are natural responses to the task of bringing new things into the world. The artist starts out with nothing, ventures into the unknown, and comes back with something. You have a right to be afraid! You have a right to doubt your abilities. You just have to muster the courage to carry on anyway.

Jealousy is often treated as the most destructive of emotions. "Compare and despair!" says the art coach Beth Pickens. "You have to make an enemy of envy . . . because it will eat you alive," says the art critic Jerry Saltz. "Some wonderful, dazzling successes are going to happen for some of the most awful, angry, undeserving writers you know," writes Anne Lamott in *Bird by Bird*. "People who are, in other words, not you."

But even jealousy can be dealt with in a healthy way. The philosopher Friedrich Nietzsche felt jealousy could be helpful to us, if we realized it was a signal that something was wrong deep inside us. Nietzsche thought that if we paid attention to envy, it could point us to the things we really want.

Don't fight your feelings. Feel them. Examine them. Use them.

WHY MAKE STUFF?

NOT NECESSARILY TO FEEL THE WAY YOU FELT WHEN YOU WERE A KID, BUT TO FEEL THE WAY YOU *WANTED* TO FEEL WHEN YOU WERE A KID...

⑦ PROBLEMS OF OUTPUT ARE PROBLEMS OF INPUT.

NO INPUT, NO OUTPUT.

Everybody knows that kids need to be exposed to lots of good stuff to grow their brains and their souls. We read books to our boys when they were in the womb. We played them music when they were babies. We took them to look at art when they were toddlers.

Humans need intellectual nourishment at every stage of their development. We take what we feed our kids seriously. But somehow, we forget that we need to feed ourselves, too.

When I have problems with my output, it's often time to work on my input. When I stall out, it's time to start taking things in:

reading books, watching movies, listening to music, going to art museums, traveling, taking people to lunch, and generally soaking up what the world has to offer. I try to be open and alert and on the lookout for that thing that will get me going again.

It can be tricky to know how much time to spend on your input and your output. “In your life, you will be evaluated by your output,” writes Ted Gioia. “But your input is just as important. If you don’t have good input, you cannot maintain good output.” The problem, Gioia notes, is that nobody manages your input, nobody cares about it, and nobody rewards you for it. But you have to be sure you make time for it, anyway. “I know for a fact I could not do what I do if I was not zealous in managing high-quality inputs into my mind every day of my life. That’s why I spend maybe two hours a day writing, but I spend three to four hours a day reading and two to three hours a day listening to music.”

Pay attention to that ratio of input to output. Double or triple the time spent on input versus the time spent on output. The first time I read Stephen King’s *On Writing* as a young person I was blown away by the fact that a writer of his prodigious output writes for about three hours in the morning, and after lunch he spends the rest of the afternoon reading. But over a hundred years ago, Anthony Trollope wrote, "Three hours a day will produce as much as a man ought to write."

Of course, the input/output ratio will be different for every creative person. It can also be seasonal, like summer and winter, with stretches of input followed by stretches of output. The ratio can also be ever-changing, depending on the demands of your day-to-day life.

If your output isn't where you want it to be, try working on your input.

"If you stuff yourself full of poems, essays, plays, stories, novels, films, comic strips, magazines, music, you automatically explode every morning like Old Faithful. I have never had a dry spell in my life, mainly because I feed myself well, to the point of bursting."

—RAY BRADBURY

KNOW WHAT YOU LIKE.

When they were younger, my kids always knew what they liked because they never cared about what they were supposed to like. For them, there was no such thing as an "important" book or a film or a piece of music. I fed them all kinds of inputs, but they didn't even try to pretend to like the things I like—in fact, sometimes they hated the things I liked just because I liked them! I took this as a very healthy sign.

I started to really envy the way my kids read books, listened to music, looked at art, and watched movies. Imagine what it would be like to really know what you like! By the time we grow up, we've been told what we're supposed to like for so long that it's easy to lose track of what it is we *really* like. We mostly like what other people like. Otherwise, we don't really know.

In order to have a point of view, artists have to know what they like. "I think a lot of what artists are doing is trying to figure out, 'What is it I really like?'" says the musician Brian Eno. "That to me is the most important question you can ask in your life, actually. It's the sort of guiding star of what you do. It sounds like a trivial question, but actually what it means is, 'What is it I really care about?'"

I often get the most blocked when I lose track of what it is that I really like. Whenever I spend a lot of time reading books that have been reviewed well by *The New York Times* or books that other people have recommended to me, I start to wander off the path of my own tastes. It can take a while to get back.

When you spend all your time ingesting things that other people like, it's easy to get to a point where you don't even know what *you* like. If you don't know what you like, how can you expect to make anything you like?

We spend so much of our input time online, having things fed to us by other people or, worse, by algorithms programmed to just give

MORE SEARCH, LESS FEED.

us more of what they think we want. The minute we open a social media app on our phone, for example, it is programmed to push at us whatever it thinks will hold our attention. We spend time in these "feeds" like pigs at a trough.

To discover the stuff you like, you can't just *feed*, you have to *search*. Your search needs to be self-directed. You can't just have things pushed *at* you; you have to pull things *toward* you.

If you're going to be online, spend less time in feeds and more time in the search box. Get outside the algorithms of the machine. Skip Google and search in online museum and library archives. Bookmark the blogs and newsletters of people who share your interests. Start digging and go deep.

Get offline as much as possible. There's so much input to be found in the real world outside of the internet. Go old school. Listen to radio shows. Browse the recently returned stacks at your local library. Buy weird old books at thrift shops. Visit a museum you've never been to. Find a good record store and chat up the clerks. Interact with real people in meatspace.

Start paying attention to who makes the stuff you like and figure out where you can find more of it. Watch the credits at the end of movies. Check the acknowledgments page and the bibliography in the backs of books you like. Actually buy or borrow albums so you can read the liner notes.

If you really don't know what you like anymore, go back to the stuff you liked when you were younger and see if you still like it. Reread, rewatch, and relisten to your old favorites. Sometimes getting back in touch with what you used to like can tell you what you really like now.

"'Attitude' was the word they used for someone who knew what they liked. They didn't want anyone to find out what they liked until it was too late."

—EVE BABITZ

COPYING IS HOW WE LEARN.

"You start when you're young and you copy.
You straight up copy."

—SHEL SILVERSTEIN

COPY WHAT YOU LOVE.

(A SMALL SAMPLING OF 3-YEAR-OLD JULES KLEON'S DRAWINGS OF EDVARD MUNCH'S THE SCREAM)

Little humans learn to be human by copying the big humans. Kids are natural-born copy machines.

I played Kraftwerk for my son Owen when he was little, and he immediately became obsessed with the band. Kraftwerk is perfect music for kids: the melodies are simple, the beats are repetitive, and they sing about real things in the world like cars, radios, trains, robots, computers, and bicycles. We listened to Kraftwerk all the time.

Owen taught himself to record music in the GarageBand software on his iPad by re-creating Kraftwerk songs. When Christmastime came around, he decided he'd remedy the fact that Kraftwerk never recorded a Christmas album by remaking their classic albums *Autobahn*, *Radio-Activity*, *Trans-Europe Express*, *The Man-Machine*, *Computer World*, and *Techno Pop* into *Christmasbahn*, *Santa Claus Activity*, *Trans-Polar Express*, *The Elf-Machine*, *Christmas World*, and *Santa Pop*. They are some of the most deranged and funniest parodies I've ever heard. I love them and listen to them every Christmas.

Owen went on to discover and copy other electronic musicians like Aphex Twin and Daft Punk. Eventually, he started writing his own original pop songs and video game music.

His progression was like my own and what I've noticed in other musicians and artists of all kinds: you start out copying your favorites, you move into parodying them, and eventually you transform them into something of your own. You begin by copying others, and if you do it well enough, eventually others wind up copying you.

EMBRACE YOUR OBSESSIONS.

In our house, we have brains that get obsessed with things. When he was little, Owen got so obsessed with combustion engines that I would let him read our car manual and old Chilton auto repair guides I checked out for him from the library. Whenever someone would visit, he'd want to look at their car engine and have me take a picture of it so he could copy out a drawing of it later.

Some parents are scared of obsessions and try to steer their kids away from them. Not me. I know that creative people aren't just fueled by their interests, but by their *obsessions*. An obsession is something that calls to you, something you cannot help but be

captured by. Obsession is what you can't stop doing. What you can't stop thinking about.

Our obsessions lead us to some of our best work. Part of the creative person's service to the world is to spend way more time than an average person thinking about a particular topic.

You often don't know why an obsession shows up or what it means. That's part of the obsession.

Obsessions can be hard to deal with. People often find themselves annoyed, frustrated, or exhausted by obsessions, wishing they would end. Obsessions can also be scary when seen from the outside—people worry that we're losing ourselves in them.

But an obsession cannot be willed or shooed away. An obsession is like a living thing. A kind of beast. It's best not to starve the beast, but to keep feeding it, so you can ride it until it's dead.

If you are obsessed with owls, for example, you go all in on owls. You read owl books. You watch owl documentaries. You go see owls at the zoo. You call up an animal rescue and ask if you can meet an owl. You sign in to Facebook just so you can join a group about local owls. You put an owl box up and watch a couple of owls raise owlets in your backyard. (Disclaimer: I have done all these things.)

Go all in, but be ready for your obsessions to leave you as quickly as they arrived and for new ones to take their place.

One day you're into owls, and the next day you're into bicycles.

And the process begins all over again.

"Talent is cheap—you have to be obsessed, otherwise you are going to give up."

—JOHN BALDESSARI

GO TO THE LIBRARY.

There is at least one place I know of where you are completely free to search for new input, know what you like, and embrace your obsessions: the public library.

I love taking my kids to the library. We are especially lucky here in Austin, Texas—we have wonderful neighborhood branch locations and a beautiful downtown library that was built when the kids were just toddlers. We have spent many a hot afternoon in the air-conditioning, reading books, listening to storytimes, and wandering the stacks.

"I used to be a librarian, you know," I once said to the boys. "Before you got fired?" Jules replied. I didn't get fired, but my first job out of college was working the reference desk in a suburban library in Cleveland. I learned so much there, and it was great training, actually, for being a parent: the librarian never asks you to be anything other than what you are—they just put you in touch with what you need. (I've often joked that if I was going to write a parenting book, I'd call it *Parent Like a Librarian*.)

The public library is a real space, away from the algorithm, where learning is self-directed, natural, and free. At the library, there is no hierarchy of expert and nonexpert—everyone in the building is a learner. The librarian provides strict rules for behavior to create an environment in which anyone can learn, but there is no curriculum, no agenda, no plan—only time, space, and resources.

The library has opening hours, but there is no schedule, no preprogrammed experience. There are no bells or bosses to interrupt you when you're in the middle of learning something.

The librarian does not demand any results from you. You are not judged or evaluated on what you know and what you don't know. There are no tests or grades.

HOW TO READ LIKE ~~AN ARTIST~~ MY KIDS:

1. READ OR HAVE SOMEONE READ TO YOU EVERY SINGLE DAY OF YOUR EXISTENCE.
2. ONLY READ BOOKS THAT YOU LIKE.
3. WHEN YOU FIND A BOOK YOU LOVE, READ IT OVER AND OVER AGAIN.
4. ALWAYS HAVE BOOKS AROUND. MAX OUT YOUR LIBRARY CARD. FILL EVERY INCH OF YOUR ROOM WITH BOOKS.
5. HAVE YOUR GIGANTIC ROOMMATE LIMIT YOUR SCREEN TIME SO THERE'S NOTHING ELSE TO DO.

At the library, you aren't limited by age or ability. You can borrow books from any section. You bump into all kinds of people, and you can learn from everyone.

The librarian is there to *serve* whoever comes through the door by connecting them with what they seek. The librarian doesn't need to know the answer to your questions; they just need to know where to look for them.

The librarian creates and maintains a collection of materials, makes spaces in which you can work and study, and curates programming tailored to the interests of the humans they serve. The librarian does not keep you under constant surveillance—as long as you are following the rules, the librarian allows you your privacy.

The library gives us the power to take learning into our own hands. The library is the true lifelong learning environment. Our relationship to the library never ends—as we grow and change, the library is there for us.

The library is a place to emulate when making your own creative spaces, and the librarian is a role model for how to approach your creative life. Be like the librarian: Do not spend time judging yourself. Simply give yourself the time, space, and resources to grow.

⑧ BORROW A KID!

A 4-YEAR-OLD WILL GET YOU UNSTUCK.

"They look at my paintings and say,
'My four-year-old could've done that.'
And I say, 'Yes. But could you?'"

—SAM MESSER

Whenever I talk to creative people who are "stuck" or "blocked," I often think they should be prescribed a session with a four-year-old.

Four-year-olds are the most "unstuck" humans around. When the cartoonist Lynda Barry started teaching at the University of Wisconsin in Madison, one thing she noticed was "how miserable the grad students were." She started a program called Drawbridge that pairs graduate students with four-year-olds as coresearchers. "What I hoped would happen was my students would learn to borrow the kids' state of mind," Barry explained. "The joy that 4-year-olds have about being alive in the world." Barry hoped the students would "learn to approach problems in a way that was less tight and focused, a way that was happier and set the conditions for discovery." And what were the four-year-olds to get out of it? Barry hoped they might "feel very excited about helping someone get their Ph.D."

I read about Barry's experiment early on in my days as a parent, and I made a point when my kids were young to bring them into the studio with me as often as possible. Every other day was "take your kid to work day," except the kids were expected to get to work, too.

MAKE AN "EXQUISITE CORPSE"

AFTER FOLDING A SHEET OF PAPER IN THIRDS, TAKE TURNS DRAWING A HEAD, A BODY, AND FEET WITHOUT LOOKING AT EACH OTHER'S DRAWINGS.

When you bring kids into the studio, you learn very quickly who should really be in charge. The illustrator Mica Angela Hendricks discovered this when she pulled out a new sketchbook one day and her four-year-old daughter insisted on drawing her own contributions. Hendricks was hesitant to share, but her daughter insisted. "If you can't share," her daughter said, "we might have to take it away."

Hendricks complied, and her daughter drew a dinosaur's body on a woman's face. Hendricks loved the drawing, and so began their collaboration: mother drawing the heads, daughter drawing the bodies. After that, each morning her daughter would ask, "Do you have any heads for me today?"

They completed "dozens and dozens" of these collaborative drawing jams. Trouble arose only when Hendricks tried to art direct her daughter and push the drawings in a certain direction. You can't really direct a four-year-old. They're not interested in your suggestions about what they should do. Best to hang back and let them rip.

"Kids' imaginations *way* outweigh a grown-up's," wrote Hendricks. She emphasized that her daughter's contributions were always better than whatever she suggested or had in her own head.

Collaborating with her daughter taught Hendricks not to be so rigid with her own drawings. "Those things you hold so dear cannot change and grow and expand unless you loosen your grip on them a little," Hendricks wrote on her blog. "If you have a preconceived notion of how something should be, YOU WILL ALWAYS BE DISAPPOINTED." If you can learn instead to just go with the flow, "something even more wonderful will come out of it."

The lessons you learn while drawing and making art with a four-year-old will stay with you long after they get bored and wander off to do something else.

"Children make up the best songs, anyway. Better than grown-ups. Kids are always working on songs and throwing them away, like little origami things or paper airplanes. They don't care if they lose it; they'll just make another one."

—TOM WAITS

TAKE LESSONS IN LOOKING.

To be with a young kid out in the world is to witness a kind of magic happening all the time. It is a magic we used to experience, when the world was all brand-new to us and we were seeing it for the first time.

"For so many years we have been learning to judge and dismiss—I know what that thing is—I've seen it a hundred times—and we've lost the complex realities, laws, and details that surround us," wrote Corita Kent and Jan Steward in their book *Learning by Heart*. "Try looking the way the child looks—as if always for the first time—and you will, I promise, feel wider awake."

Hanging out with a young kid can teach us to see in that childlike way again.

Once my kids were old enough to walk, one of my favorite things to do was to let them lead me around an art museum. Kids make perfect museum guides because they have no preconceived notions about what is or isn't art. They're just drawn to what they like. If they can't read yet, even better, because they can't be influenced by the labels next to the paintings telling them why they're so important to look at.

Kids naturally go through a museum in the way the more sophisticated museumgoers I know go about it: ignoring the labels, letting their attention be captured, and seeing with fresh eyes.

The greatest thing looking at art can do for you is help you see your everyday world in a new light, from a new perspective. Kids in a museum often skip the "looking at art" step and go straight to the "seeing everyday life as art." I took Owen to an outdoor sculpture garden once, and he spent the whole time at the entrance gate, squealing with glee at the cars zipping by on the road. (What are cars, after all, but moving sculptures?) At the Blanton Museum of Art here in Austin, my boys would inevitably get down on the floor and admire the neon exit signs next to the doorways.

EXIT
EXIT

When you talk to kids about art, you quickly realize how little you actually know about it and how much you've never bothered to articulate. You also discover things you've never fully realized before.

"Talking to my kids about what we're looking at helps clarify my thinking," writes the novelist Rumaan Alam. "I have to articulate, in terms a kid can comprehend, what I see or feel or think about a piece of art. I find I don't rush to my own judgment, even if I think I've already made that judgment."

Talking about art is fun, but my best memories of museum visits are bringing pencils and sketchbooks and drawing with my kids. Learning to look together, wordlessly, side by side.

Lessons in looking need not be limited to the museum, of course. Getting down on the floor and playing with a kid will give you a fresh perspective on life. A quick stroll around a city block or a trip to the grocery store will provide you with a week's worth of inspiration.

Borrow a kid and let them teach you how to be alive in the world. Their parents will gladly accept the break.

WHEN	INSTEAD OF	TRY
YOU MEET A KID	"WHAT DO YOU WANT TO BE WHEN YOU GROW UP?"	"WHAT DO YOU LOVE TO DO?"
THEY SHARE SOMETHING THEY MADE	"WHAT IS IT?"	"TELL ME ABOUT THIS!"
THEY LIKE SOMETHING YOU DON'T	"I DON'T LIKE THIS."	"TELL ME WHAT YOU LIKE ABOUT THIS!"
THEY COME TO YOU WITH A PROBLEM	"YOU SHOULD JUST..."	"THAT SOUNDS HARD. HOW CAN I HELP?"

* OR ANYONE ELSE ** OR ANYTHING ELSE

VISIT THE CHILDREN'S SECTION.

"I like kids' work more than work by real artists any day."

—JEAN-MICHEL BASQUIAT

If you don't have kids in your life, or they're unavailable, or you simply can't stand being around them at the moment, there's another handy way to access the world of childhood: visit the children's section of your local library or bookstore.

In her book *Why You Should Read Children's Books, Even Though You Are So Old and Wise*, the author Katherine Rundell makes the case that reading children's books "offers to help us refind things we may not even know we have lost."

"When you read children's books, you are given the space to read again as a child," Rundell writes. "To find your way back, back to the time when new discoveries came daily and when the world was colossal, before your imagination was trimmed and neatened, as if it were an optional extra."

Rundell emphasizes that reading kids' books is not about hiding or escaping the adult world, but seeking out new things within it. "Read a children's book to remember what it was to long for impossible and perhaps-not-impossible things," Rundell writes. "See the world with double eyes: your own, and those of your childhood self."

T o

be

a

Teacher

remain

a Student

The children's section isn't just a place of dreams, fantasy, and imagination; it's also a playful place to learn serious new things.

"I was never a diligent student," says the *Jeopardy!* champion James Holzhauer. "I have a strategy of reading children's books to gain knowledge. I've found that in an adult reference book, if it's not a subject I'm interested in, I just can't get into it."

The children's section, on the other hand, is a place Holzhauer discovered "to get books tailored to make things interesting for uninterested readers."

If you can't borrow a kid, borrow their books.

"If you eat enough books, you start pooping out words."

—CAITLIN MORAN

BE A CURIOUS ELDER.

"To see is to forget the name of the thing one sees."

—PAUL VALÉRY

The filmmaker John Waters likes to joke that he has "Youth Spies" that keep him supplied with new information and trends that nobody his age has heard of yet. "I'm still interested in life," Waters says. "I don't think it was better when I was young. I think the kids that are fifteen and getting into trouble are having as much fun as I did."

Waters is what I call a Curious Elder. A Curious Elder is someone who manages to retain their curiosity as they age. They stay interested in what young people are up to.

The Curious Elder isn't interested in judging youth. They're interested in learning from them. For the Curious Elder, "The kids are alright!" isn't an observation; it's an attitude. The Curious Elder assumes that they have as much to learn from young people as young people have to learn from them. The Curious Elder doesn't try to be hip, or act young, or participate in youth culture; they're just open to understanding people younger than they are and seeing from the perspective they have to offer.

As you age, become a Curious Elder. You won't always understand what's going on. It's actually a good thing if you are confused by young people and what they're up to.

EMBRACE
BEWILDERMENT

“If we can understand our children, we’re all screwed,” said the cybernetician Stafford Beer to musician Brian Eno.

Sometimes people younger than you will scare you, shake you up, or downright mystify you.

“Revel in your mystification,” Eno suggests. “Read it as a sign of a healthy future. Whatever happens next, it won’t be what you expected. If it is what you expected, it isn’t what’s happening next.”

The Curious Elder remains connected to the future by connecting with the youth of the present.

No matter what age you are, you can stay curious and share your curiosity with other people of all ages. You can be the Youth Spy for someone older and the Curious Elder for someone younger.

> **“When does a person stop being a child? Can you say that a child is ever entirely eliminated from an adult?”**
>
> **—WALT DISNEY**

9
NOTHING IS WASTED.

CREATIVITY IS THE RESIDUE OF TIME WASTED.

My kids rewired my sense of time. Our time together is not linear or uniform—it doesn't move in a straight line, and it passes by at different speeds. Some days drag by with mistakes and dead ends and nothing to show for the hours spent. Other days fly by in a flurry of activity. Months and years are even slipperier. The kids grow and I grow, but a feeling of progress is elusive—the rhythm of our growth together feels more like a cycle of seasons on a planet, turning in a spiral of forward and retrograde motion.

For most of human history, we measured time by natural rhythms: heartbeats, sunrises and sunsets, moon phases, and the passing of the seasons. There are no straight lines in nature, and nature's rhythms aren't straight either—they're circular, fluid, and continuous, without edges, and without clean-cut beginnings or endings.

We invented clocks and calendars so we could slice and dice time into quantified chunks: seconds, minutes, hours, days, months, years, decades. This is the time of our modern world, designed for the values of efficiency and industry. In this world, time is money—a substance that is scarce, precious, and valuable.

Hanging out with little kids put me in a different mode of time, one that wasn't so connected to the productivity of the clock and the calendar. "Time passed extremely slowly, as time should pass, with the days lingering and long, spacious and free as the summers of childhood," as Edward Abbey wrote in *Desert Solitaire*. "There was time enough for once to do nothing, or next to nothing." My kids and I had a lot of time to waste, and we wasted it deliciously, together.

To waste time in the modern world is considered the greatest of sins, and idleness is looked upon with suspicion. To be thought of as productive, one needs to look busy. But you will not always look busy when you're being creative. In fact, if you check in on creative people at different moments in the day, it will look like they are doing absolutely nothing, or doing the kinds of things kids get yelled at for in the classroom: daydreaming, fidgeting, doodling, or staring out the window.

There is simply no way to know by the looks of things whether anything is actually getting done. In the course of one's day, month, or year, it's sometimes impossible to know what's a waste of time and what's not. Quite often, what seemed like a waste at the time turns out not to have been a waste at all.

This is why it is critical to give yourself time to do nothing. Jenny Odell, author of *How to Do Nothing*, gives her students this advice every quarter: "Leave yourself twice as much time as you think you need for a project, knowing that half of that may not look like 'making' anything at all."

Give yourself time to waste. Forget all your ideas about "efficiency." Work as slowly or as quickly as you want to. Resist the urge to get back to work, to stop idling, to find something to do with yourself.

It's your time. Waste it all you want, with all your heart.

you

are

a spacecraft

on

a trip to Pluto.

and

you have time

BOREDOM IS A PIT STOP.

I am struck over and over by how many artists can trace their creative lives back to childhood boredom.

"I think I turned out the way I did because I was so bored," said the musician Trent Reznor about his childhood in Pennsylvania. "There weren't a lot of things to distract you, so you'd end up turning inward."

"We had the freedom to get bored," said the author Cressida Cowell of her childhood. "Boredom is very good for creativity, for it forces you to think up your own entertainment and discover something to do."

"There's nothing like boredom to make you write," Agatha Christie wrote in her autobiography. Christie was homeschooled until the age of sixteen and was gifted plenty of time to be "gloriously idle." Because she was left alone so much, she had to learn how to entertain herself. "So by the time I was sixteen or seventeen," she wrote, "I'd written quite a number of short stories and one long, dreary novel."

We hate being bored, which is why it's so valuable to us: Our brains will do anything to avoid it. Being bored becomes a spur for creative action.

The trouble now is that we live in an age in which we never give ourselves the chance to be bored. All the entertainment we could ever dream of is at our fingertips, waiting on the phone in our pocket.

"Boredom [is] a pit stop on the way to figuring out what fascinates you."

—ASTRA TAYLOR

"Gadgetry means never having to feel that pain, or that spur," wrote Nicholas Carr. "The web expands to fill all boredom. That's dangerous for everyone, but particularly so for kids, who, without boredom's spur, may never discover what in themselves or in their surroundings is most deeply engaging to them."

It's important to allow ourselves to feel bored.

"Boredom is your window," wrote the poet Joseph Brodsky. "Once this window opens, don't try to shut it; on the contrary, throw it wide open."

If you stare out the window of boredom long enough, it will show you something interesting.

**"It takes a lot of time to be a genius.
You have to sit around so much, doing nothing,
really doing nothing."**

—GERTRUDE STEIN

IT'S OKAY TO QUIT.

Some people tell kids, "Winners never quit and quitters never win."

Not me. Such commonplace wisdom does not apply to artists.

There is no winning in the creative life. You are not in a race; you are on a journey. You can go as fast or as slow as you want to. There's no stopping when you're running a race, but when you're on a journey, it's good to stop, take a break, look around, and get your bearings.

Stopping for a while is not the same as quitting. You can stop and reserve the right to start again.

GAME
OVER
TRY AGAIN
QUIT

But it's also perfectly okay to quit.

"What a waste of talent!" we cry when somebody quits. But talent only gets us so far for so long. If you want to get somewhere, you must persist and persevere, and to do that you must have the desire to keep going. If you follow your true interests and your curiosity, the desire to keep going will be there.

We're afraid to quit because we're so afraid of loss—we can't see what might be gained by quitting. But when we quit the things we don't love, we clear space for new things to take their place.

Sometimes when we quit things we realize just how much they mean to us. We return to the things we've quit with a fresh enthusiasm and perspective.

Eddie Van Halen's mother was really angry at him when he quit the piano to focus on the guitar. Even after he became a rock star, she thought he was wasting his talent. But those piano lessons weren't wasted: a half decade into Van Halen's career, he got out a synthesizer and composed the song "Jump," which became the band's biggest hit.

"When you let go of something, it will still be there for you when you need it," wrote Gordon MacKenzie in *Orbiting the Giant*

Hairball. "But because you have stopped clinging, you will have freed yourself up to tap into other possibilities."

Nothing is wasted. Let yourself quit what truly isn't working for you! Learn to let go of things that no longer matter.

Quitting is a skill that can be learned in miniature. An easy way to train yourself to learn the value of quitting things is to stop reading books that you don't like. (Hopefully not this book!) Give a book fifty pages, and if it's not doing anything for you, put it down and find another one. Every hour you spend inching through a boring book is an hour you could've spent sailing through a brilliant one.

The same goes for the bigger things in life—quitting the little things trains you to quit the big things. To respond to what's really not working for you, to be flexible, and to correct course.

"We give things up when we believe we can change; we give up when we believe we can't."

—ADAM PHILLIPS

GOLDILOCKS theory OF CREATIVITY

LIFE IS TOO DEPRESSING TO WORK

LIFE IS JUST DEPRESSING ENOUGH THAT WORK IS A HAPPY ALTERNATIVE

LIFE IS TOO GOOD TO WORK

DON'T THROW YOURSELF OUT THE WINDOW.

My wife, Meghan, is the oldest of four kids. Her parents, when they were on baby number four, were once asked at a birthing class if they had any advice for the rookie parents. My father-in-law stood up and addressed the group.

"Look, at some point, you're going to want to throw the baby out the window," he said to the widening eyes of everyone in the room. "And that's okay! The important thing is that you don't."

Then he sat back down.

I'd Like
A
lighter
way to
escape
than
tumbling out of a window

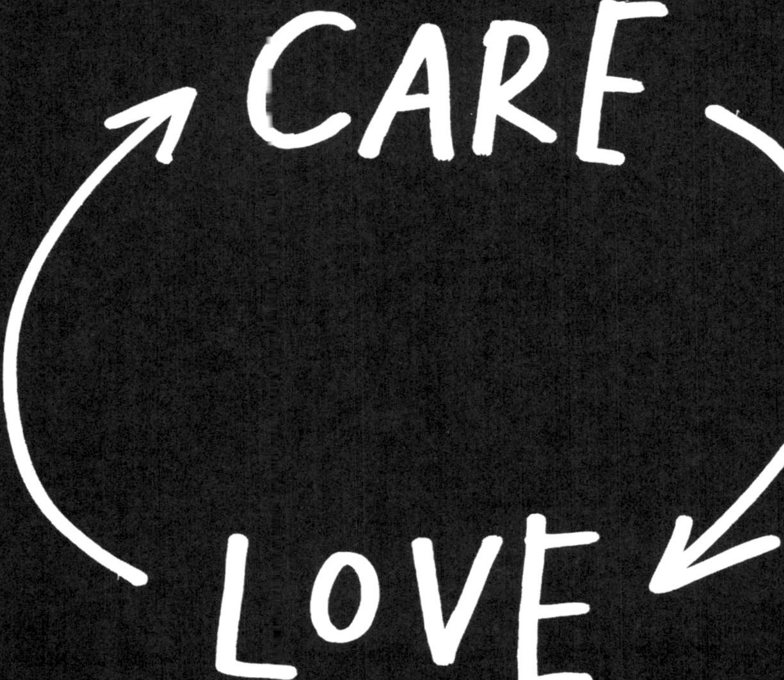

CARE

LOVE

I've told that story dozens of times to other parents. It's still the greatest parenting advice I've ever heard.

It doubles as life advice, of course: don't throw yourself out the window.

The life of an artist is like any other life: It will have its ups and downs. There will be times when you don't even like yourself, when you will wish to get as far away from yourself as possible.

But you don't have to love or even like yourself all the time. All you have to do is care for yourself. Go through the motions of care: give yourself grace, clean up your messes, and do the thankless maintenance work that must be done.

There will be days when you want to throw yourself out the window. That's okay! The important thing is that you don't.

"You do not even have to believe in yourself or your work. You have to keep yourself open and aware directly to the urges that motivate you. Keep the channel open."

—MARTHA GRAHAM

(10) YOU DON'T NEED A VISION.

PUT THE FUTURE BEHIND YOU.

I take a look at the world and it's very difficult to picture the kind of future my kids are going to live in.

I think of the motivational slogans: *Put the past behind you. The future is bright ahead*.

Is it? In my lifetime, it seems like the past keeps coming back and the future keeps falling behind.

When we talk about time, we usually refer to the past as being *behind* us and the future being *ahead* of us. This space-time arrangement seems so totally natural to us, it's hard to imagine what it would be like to think otherwise.

Years ago, I read about the Aymara, a tribe of Indigenous people in South America who have a way of thinking about time that's the complete reverse of our own. They refer to the future as "back" or "behind" time, and the past as "front" time. When they speak about the past, they gesture *ahead* of them, and when they speak about the future, they gesture *behind* them.

The reason they point ahead when talking about the past is that the past is *known*—it has already happened, therefore, it's in front of you, where you can see it. The future, on the other hand, is *unknown*—it hasn't happened yet, so it's behind you, where you can't see it.

I read about this almost fifteen years ago and it still blows my mind.

The past is in front of us. The future is behind us.

I decided way back then that whenever I started getting too worried or confused—or too certain!—about the future, I would steal some inspiration from the Aymara.

When thinking about the future becomes overwhelming, I put it behind me, where it belongs. I focus on the past and that tiny sliver of now we call "the present," which is right in front of me.

THE PAST

HAS ALREADY HAPPENED SO IT IS

IN FRONT OF YOU

WHERE YOU CAN SEE IT

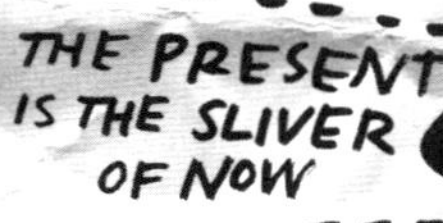

WHERE
THEY MEET

THE FUTURE

HAS YET TO HAPPEN, SO IT IS

BEHIND YOU

WHERE YOU CAN'T SEE IT

WORK WITH WHAT'S IN FRONT OF YOU.

My son once dunked a soccer ball into a basketball hoop and shouted "Touchdown!" There is no question he is my kid. I have a filmmaker friend, on the other hand, whose son is a total jock. We joke all the time about how he is living the dream of other dads, but how totally ill-equipped he is for it. He's a good dad, though, because he works with what's in front of him: he shows up at games and practices and he loves his kid and he doesn't ask him to be anything else.

Dads often get weird visions about what it's going to be like to be a dad. They get pictures in their heads about all the things they're going to do with their kids and all the things they're going to teach them. I see creative people do this, too. They have a big vision of what their life is going to be like, and when the reality doesn't match the vision, they feel like a failure.

Thought leaders and inspirational gurus are constantly telling us about the importance of *having a vision*. I'm a fan of Arnold Schwarzenegger, but he is constantly going on and on about how he *visualized* his way to success and how important it is for people who want to be successful to have a *vision*. "Turn your vision into reality!" he says. His message is that you have to see clearly what you want before you can take the steps to get it. "Vision is everything," he says. "You must be able to visualize your end goal for it to be real."

And this talk of vision sounds very inspiring—it really does pump you up!—but for many of the creative people I look up to, it would have been almost useless advice.

The artist ventures into the unknown, making and doing things that no one has ever seen before. There is rarely any clear path available to envision for such a creative life.

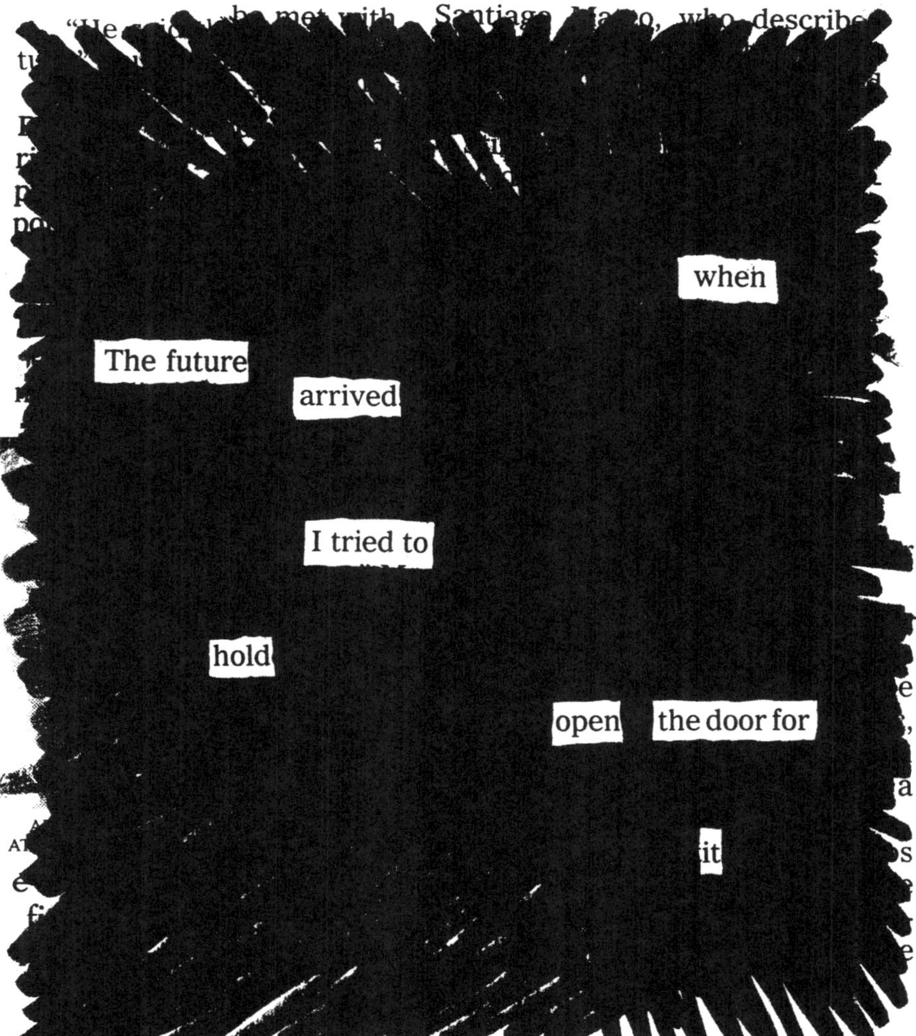
when
The future
arrived
I tried to
hold
open
the door for
it

Arnold's success is remarkable, but it's important to remember that for each thing he wanted to be, there was a path he could visualize to get there. Being the best bodybuilder, the most famous actor in Hollywood, the governor of California—Arnold could see these goals clearly and figure out how to get there because they already existed in the world.

I am a person who does not really know what I want to do or who I want to be. This has been the case for many years. I don't have any huge goals or a grand vision for my life. I just try to do the work that's in front of me.

It's worth pointing out that there are plenty of successful creative people—maybe even a *majority*—who had no clear vision or idea of what they wanted to do with themselves, let alone any goals or ideas about how to get there!

"I've never planned anything," said the filmmaker Werner Herzog. "I haven't had any career at all. I only have a life." (Sometimes I can hear Herzog and Schwarzenegger battling in my head with their respective German and Austrian accents.)

You might be tempted to take Arnold's advice: to visualize your goals, make a plan, and see it through. You might even have a clear vision for what you want to do and who you want to be. If you do, that's great, and you should go for it. (I envy you!)

But I would discourage you from clinging to your visions *too* tightly, because your visions can blind you to what's actually in front of you—who you really are and what you really can be. Sometimes we get so focused on our vision that we simply miss a lot of the good around us. The stuff we could really use. We miss out on opportunities. We get driven crazy by the mismatch between our vision and our reality. The vision becomes more destructive than creative.

We don't talk very often about the *danger* of visions. Visions can be very powerful, but visions can create a kind of *inflexibility* in us. Chasing after our visions can cause us to bulldoze through reality with blinders on. History is full of people with a vision who left a wide path of destruction in their wake.

If you don't have a picture in your head of how things are supposed to be, you're less likely to be frustrated by or distracted from what's actually happening in front of you.

I take great inspiration from people with a condition called aphantasia. People with aphantasia are the very small portion of the population who cannot make pictures in their heads. If you ask them to close their eyes and visualize an apple, they don't see an image—their "mind's eye" is blind. (People with aphantasia often discover their condition only when they realize that when people ask them to "picture" something, they aren't speaking in metaphor.)

You would think an inability to make pictures in your head would be a huge disability when it comes to making pictures on paper or on the screen . . . and you would be totally wrong! People with aphantasia can be found in all the creative industries. Ed Catmull, the former president and cofounder of the animation studio Pixar, has written at length about his own aphantasia and the animators with aphantasia he's discovered in his company. Their difference does not preclude them at all from doing creative work. Far from it.

"If you open your eyes and you take out a pencil and a pad, how many people can draw what they see?" Catmull asks. "The answer is a very small number, so if you can't draw what is front of you then why would we expect that you would be able to draw what you visualize?"

Like many differences, in the right context, aphantasia becomes a superpower. The artist with aphantasia doesn't see what they're

looking for until they create it, which means they'll often find in their creations things they didn't know they were looking for.

People with aphantasia present us with a different model for living and growing. You could spend a bunch of time trying to come up with some kind of vision for your creative life to chase after, or you could start working with what's in front of you and see what appears. Instead of sitting down at your desk and starting out with a clear picture of what you want to do, you can start pushing materials around, sketching, tinkering, improvising, exploring, and experimenting.

The materials at hand are the only materials you ever have. To not start out with a vision in your head means you can really see what's in front of you and then figure out what to do with it. If you start with no preconceived notion of what things are going to look like, you can remain flexible and open. You can discover things that are beyond what you or anyone else could've pictured.

"[It's] like driving at night in the fog. You can only see as far as your headlights, but you can make the whole trip that way."

—E. L. DOCTOROW

GET BEYOND YOUR IMAGINATION.

When I think about what's next for me and for my kids, it's simply beyond my imagination. I'm okay with that.

We speak of the imagination as a boundless place of endless possibilities—but even the imagination has its limits. At many points in our lives, we hit a spot where we simply can't imagine what we should do next. We lose the thread; we lose our energy; we sometimes lose our whole sense of who we are.

Everything is temporary. The only constant in the creative life

A PRAYER TO the ANGEL OF UNCERTAINTY

"PLEASE DON'T LET ME SCREW IT UP, BUT JUST SCREW IT UP A LITTLE BIT. (JUST ENOUGH TO MAKE IT INTERESTING.)"

—SALLY MANN

is change. Loving and caring for yourself and your loved ones is a lifelong task that requires endless adjustments and tweaking.

What worked yesterday might not work today. What works today might not work tomorrow.

Whenever you think you have things figured out, you can be sure that bewilderment lies ahead.

No matter what you think is going to happen next, what actually happens next will probably surprise you.

The artist's job is to take us all beyond our wildest imaginations. To show us things we've never seen and to boldly go where none of us has even thought about going before. If you're going to do that, you have to venture into unknown territory, to explore what's not on any map, to go places you might not even want to go.

Forget whatever you had in mind. Go back to that childlike mode of *not knowing*. Give yourself the time, space, and materials you need. Play hide-and-seek with the world and all its burdens and responsibilities. Make a big pile of imperfect things. Believe in magic. Think outside your head. Feed your obsessions. Borrow a kid if you need to. Pretend it's a comedy. Keep your sense of humor. *Don't call it art: just make stuff.*

ONE DAY YOU'LL MAKE SOMETHING AND YOU WON'T KNOW WHAT IT IS. IT'LL BE SOMETHING YOU'VE NEVER SEEN BEFORE. YOU MIGHT NOT EVEN LIKE IT AT FIRST, BUT IT GIVES YOU GOOSEBUMPS. THERE'S SOMETHING TO IT. YOU'LL WANT TO SHOW IT TO SOMEBODY ELSE, SOMEBODY YOU TRUST. THEY WON'T KNOW WHAT IT IS, EITHER, AT FIRST. YOU'LL BOTH STARE AT IT FOR A BIT, SCRATCHING YOUR HEADS.

WHAT IS THIS THING YOU MADE?

YOU MIGHT CALL IT ART.

SOFT FUR
EARS
TREE
SHARP BEAK
AUSTIN
EARLY PLASTIC, BATTERY-POWERED TOY ROBOT
THE LEGS ARE
INK
All You need to do is turn the page.
THE END

YOUR SPEED
UPERHEROOWEN
MACHINEMACHINEMACHINE
-IAGIN-OF-A-BUS
GASTAIK
YOUR SPEED

WHAT NOW?

"You just gotta keep making s—t up, scribbling—like sitting down and drawing with my kids. It reminds me to do that in my songs. It doesn't matter if it's good or bad. I think it looks great. Let's hang it on the refrigerator."

—JEFF TWEEDY

- ☐ HIRE A KID TO TEACH YOU TO PLAY.
- ☐ REWATCH/REREAD/RELISTEN TO YOUR CHILDHOOD FAVORITES.
- ☐ ACQUIRE SOME NEW TOYS.
- ☐ SCHEDULE PLAYTIME.
- ☐ ASK YOURSELF: "WHEN I WAS A KID, WHAT MADE HOURS PASS LIKE MINUTES?"
- ☐ JUST GO EASY ON YOURSELF!
- ☐ GIVE A COPY OF THIS BOOK TO SOMEONE WHO NEEDS TO READ IT.
- ☐ SIGN UP FOR MY FREE WEEKLY NEWSLETTER AT AUSTINKLEON.COM.

BOOKS ARE MADE OUT OF BOOKS...

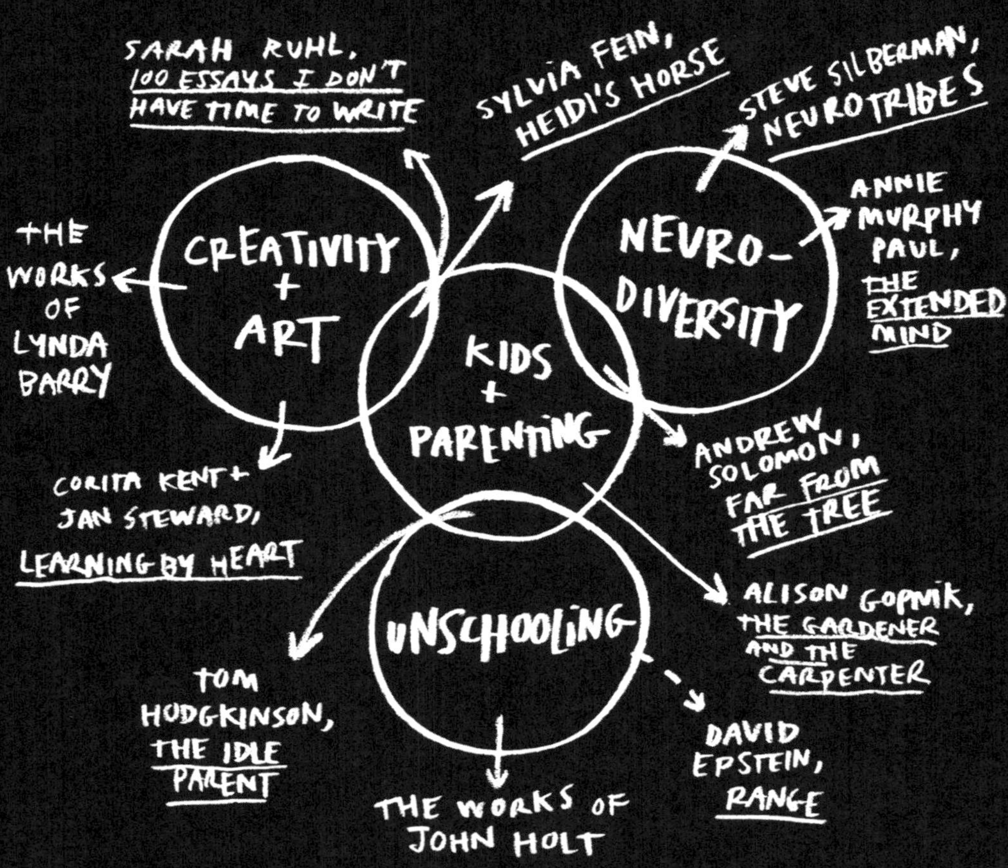

... AND OTHER THINGS.

- *AMERICAN ELF: THE COLLECTED SKETCHBOOK DIARIES OF JAMES KOCHALKA*
- *BEAUTY IS EMBARRASSING*, A 2012 DOCUMENTARY ABOUT WAYNE WHITE
- TOVE JANSSON'S *MOOMIN* COMICS
- "SAUL STEINBERG WITH HIS SIX-YEAR-OLD SELF," PHOTO BY EVELYN HOFER
- *A BRIEF HISTORY OF JOHN BALDESSARI*, SHORT FILM
- "PLAY IT LIKE YOUR HAIR'S ON FIRE" 2002 GQ PROFILE OF TOM WAITS BY ELIZABETH GILBERT
- THE TV SHOW *BLUEY*
- FLEA'S MONOLOGUE IN *THE OTHER F WORD*
- SU SHI'S 1,000-YEAR-OLD POEM, "ON THE BIRTH OF HIS SON"

THE ADVENTURES OF O-BOT

I USED TO DRAW OWEN AS A ROBOT IN MY DIARY AND RECORD THE FUNNY THINGS HE SAID...

MAMA! IT'S A FULL MOON TONIGHT!
REALLY? HOW DO YOU KNOW?
I LOOKED OUT THE WINDOW!

PAPA WHERE ARE YOU FLYING?
NEW MEXICO
BUT PAPA! YOU DON'T SPEAK SPANISH!

WELL, PAPA'S GONE NOW, SO I HAVE TO WRITE BOOKS AND MAKE MONEY.

HELL CAT?
owen reads the dictionary

I'M WORRIED I'LL RUN OUT OF ROOM IN MY BRAIN.
YOU SHUT THE DOOR! I'M WORKING, HERE!
THE BOOK WOULD BE CALLED BIG TO SMALL.
ON THE FIRST PAGE WOULD BE THE UNIVERSE...
ON THE LAST PAGE WOULD BE MAYBE A MICROBE OR AN ATOM...
IT WOULD BE A LONG BOOK!

HOW DO FISHES LEARN TO SWIM..
IF THEY DON'T GO TO SWIM SCHOOL?

JULES REALLY WORKS HARD ON HIS DRAWINGS
I THINK HE THINKS DRAWINGS CAN CHANGE THE WORLD!

AWWW MY DREAMS ARE NOT COMING REAL!!!

IF I WAS BUYING YOU, I'D PRESS CANCEL!
AT THE POOL...

OOH LOOK! MONEY!
WHAT WOULD YOU DO IF YOU HAD MONEY?
I WOULD SCRATCH OFF MAGIC SPELLS!

PAPA I LOVE YOU
AW I LOVE YOU TOO, SON
HOMEWORK
PERFORM AN ACT OF KINDNESS

THANK YOU

Owen and Jules Kleon. Many readers have commented how lucky you two are to have me as a dad, when it's actually the other way around. You changed my life for the better, and the world is better with you in it. Keep making stuff.

Meghan Kleon, who did so much work on this book at every single stage that she deserves a coauthor credit. Every writer needs an editor, and I'm lucky to be married to a great one. (I thought it'd be easier this time around, and I'm sorry—maybe next time!)

Ted Weinstein, for his guidance and for always remembering to get the money.

Marian Lizzi, Shannon Plunkett, Sabrey Manning, and the rest of the fine folks at Tarcher. It's been a pleasure.

James Flynn and Matt Thomas for the phone calls. Alan Jacobs for the texts. Marty Butler and Hank Kidwell for the bike rides.

Lynda Barry for giving me the idea to turn my kids into my teachers. Nina Katchadourian for introducing me to *Survive the Savage Sea*. Mandy Brown for introducing me to *The Comedy of Survival*. Ryan Holiday for the idea of "a parenting book in disguise." Roberto Greco, Lori Pickert, and Astra Taylor for exposing me to the world of unschooling. Drew Dernavich for his pile of imperfect things. Andy Goldsworthy for his art in the Presidio in San Francisco, including "Earth Wall," which is pictured at the beginning of the "Believe in Magic" chapter. Fiona Apple for the "Eureka!" moment and the best record released during lockdown. Walter Martin for his radio show and his song "The Soldier," which I was listening to when I came up with the ending. Brian Eno for his ideas about art and play.

Finally, my readers all over the world, with a special shout-out to my paid newsletter subscribers, who buy me the time in between books to experiment, fool around, and play like a kid.

UNO!
PAPA
Oh! No! i'THIK iM' POOPING iN my PANTS!
FART!

ABOUT THE AUTHOR

© Clayton Cubitt

Austin Kleon is the *New York Times* bestselling author of *Steal Like an Artist*, *Show Your Work!*, *Keep Going*, and *Newspaper Blackout*. His books have been translated into over thirty languages and have sold over two million copies worldwide. He lives in Austin, Texas. To keep in touch, join the hundreds of thousands of readers who subscribe to his weekly newsletter at **austinkleon.com**.

OVER 2 MILLION COPIES SOLD.

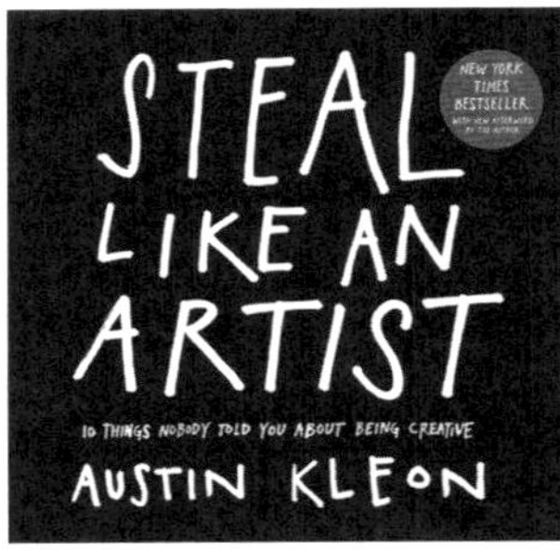

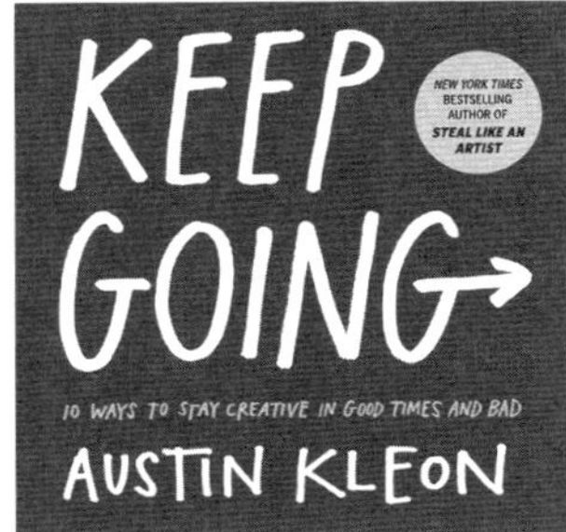

AUSTINKLEON.COM

HOME SWEET HOME
NOOO
LITTLE PIGS!
NO
i LOVE TO WORK EASY.
CREEPY PLACE
KEEP OUT!